LIVING WITH DRAGONS

G. Scott Leis
Copyright © 2013 G. Scott Leis

All rights reserved.

ISBN-10: 0692027866
ISBN-13: 978-0692027868

LIVING WITH DRAGONS

WITH THE KOREAN MARINES IN VEITNAM

AUGUST 1968 – MAY 1970

G. SCOTT LEIS

Dedication

This book is dedicated to those I served with, both USMC and ROKMC. You are all my brothers-in-arms.

I told my story as I remember it. I have forgotten some names and have taken the liberty of changing others.

Chapter 1
Yellow Footprints

Rain had formed a drop on the tip of my nose that refused to drop. I wanted ever so badly to scratch my nose. But I mustn't. I was standing on painted yellow footprints in a line with nine other guys. It was night, and we were standing in the rain at the position of "ATTENTION," heals together, toes at a 45° angle, back straight and eyes straight ahead. A man in a green raincoat wearing a Smokey Bear hat with its own fitted clear plastic covering was screaming at the guy next to me. The Smokey Bear, who had introduced himself as Drill Instructor Sergeant Hunt, had been telling the ten of us how he sincerely hoped that the rest of his platoon was not as worthless as us, when the guy to my left forgot the "eyes straight ahead" rule and glanced over at the DI. Sergeant Hunt's reaction was immediate. He ran over, and with his chest within two inches of the scared recruit, shouted at him,

"WHY ARE YOU LOOKING AT ME YOU PIECE OF SH*T? YOU DON'T LIKE ME, DO YOU SCUMBALL?"

It is never polite or wise to tell someone you fear that you don't like them. So the recruit, remembering that the first and last word out of our "filthy" mouths is always "Sir," replied,

"Sir, I do like you Sir."

The D.I. leaned into the tall recruit's chest and screamed,

"I CAN'T HEAR YOU LADY!"

The near-panicked recruit screamed back,

"SIR, I DO LIKE YOU SIR!"

His answer only enraged Drill Instructor Sergeant Hunt even more. He was only about 5'10" or so, a good three inches shorter than the recruit. Bouncing up and down on the balls of his feet, he yelled in the Private's face,

"YOU CALLED ME A EWE! DO I LOOK LIKE A SHEEP, PRIVATE? YOU LIKE ME? YOU WANT TO FU*K ME, PRIVATE? WELL DO YOU, YOU SLIMY PILE OF SH*T?"

An itchy nose was the least of my problems right now.

I was grateful when more buses pulled up with more recruits to spread the abuse around. Group abuse was bad, individual abuse was much worse. While we waited for more buses, the rain, and Sergeant Hunt's verbal flogging, mixed with rules, never abated. He had just told us that we were never to refer to ourselves as "I," but as "The Private," when he caught another recruit looking at him. The procedure was the same as for the first "looker." The recruit had heard the wrong answer to, "YOU DON'T LIKE ME, DO YOU SCUMBALL?" So he answered,

"SIR! NO SIR! THE PRIVATE DOES NOT LIKE THE DRILL INSTRUCTOR, SIR!"

That apparently wasn't the right thing to say either.

"WELL!" Drill Instructor Sergeant Hunt snarled, "SO YOU DON'T LIKE ME! WELL, I DON'T LIKE YOU EITHER YOU SLIMY TURD!" With a stiff index finger, he tapped the guy's chest, "I WILL REMEMER YOU FU*KWAD! IF YOU DON'T GET YOUR SH*T TOGETHER, I WILL TEAR YOU A NEW A*SHOLE! WHAT'S YOUR NAME, SCUMBALL?"

Pretty much a lose-lose situation, I realized.

I had been raised in a Christian home on a 3000 acre farm and ranch in northeast Colorado. I only had my mouth washed out a few times before I learned that "dirty language" is not acceptable. Almost everyone I knew followed the same principle. I had not heard as many "bad" words in a month as I heard in one minute from Sergeant Hunt. My mother would not approve of the company I was keeping.

My cream colored corduroy pants and untucked white shirt were plastered on my skinny six foot, 155 pound frame. My long blond hair was matted and covered the top of my glasses. It had been raining since I, and three other Marine Corps recruits, had landed in San Diego on a night flight from Denver. Although it didn't seem necessary, the airport Marine Corporal had insisted that we stand in the rain at the bus stop. We had discussed the airport desk Marine's attitude and decided that maybe he was just having a bad day. After standing in the rain for about twenty minutes, a green Marine Corps bus pulled up. A Corporal in green utilities got off the bus and started screaming at us because we didn't have enough sense to get out of the rain. With a few choice words, he ordered us on the bus. Trying to please, we rushed onto the bus and took a seat. That didn't calm him down a bit,

"YOU SORRY PUKES ARE DRIPPING WATER IN MY BUS!"

One of the other guys started to explain that the Corporal in the airport made us stand outside in the rain. That only keyed an outburst personally directed at our advocate. The Corporal yelled at us all the way until we stopped. As soon as the driver opened the door, Sergeant Hunt burst in like he was a hungry coyote, and we were fat chickens. As we scrambled over each other to get off the bus, Sergeant Hunt, the Corporal and maybe even the bus driver were screaming at us. We ran over to join the half-a-dozen other recruits that were already standing on the yellow footprints. We were the first recruits of Platoon "One Fifty Two."

"What are the odds," I thought, "of the first four Marines I met all having a bad day?" I took a silent vow to never speak to anyone, other than a recruit, unless it was absolutely necessary.

After a few more buses arrived, the yellow footprints were full, and we formed a line going into a small room with half a dozen barber chairs. Sergeant Hunt stood at the door and made sure there was never an empty chair. I stood next in line. I didn't have to wait long. It only took each barber about thirty seconds per haircut, and I ran forward to an open chair and sat down. The barber asked if I had any moles or warts. I replied that I didn't, and with seven or eight sweeps of the electric razor, my long, wet blond hair lay in my lap.

We were herded into a large building with long tables that had cardboard boxes lined up on them. A different, but no less abusive Smokey Bear, told us to strip down naked and pack all of our "slimy civilian crap" in the boxes before us. *I feel that at that moment, after I had packed my clothes, was a turning point in my life. Stripped of everything I knew before that moment was almost like a new birth. The first and second life resemble each other only in that I came in bald and naked.* We addressed the box to our home, and moved on, naked, to different tables to receive our first issue of clothing.

The first thing they gave us was a large green canvas sea bag. Thankfully, the next items we received were our white boxer shorts, white tee shirts and our green wool socks. We were ordered to put on a pair of shorts, a tee shirt and a pair of socks and pack the rest in our sea bag. We were quickly measured and issued: green utility shirts with "USMC" stamped on the left breast pocket, trousers, caps (hereafter referred to as "covers") and a yellow sweat shirt with a large red Marine Corps' "Eagle, Globe and Anchor" printed on the front. As we moved down the line, we received our boots, a pair of tennis shoes and toilet articles. After we had all our clothes, we were given the order to get dressed in our trousers, yellow sweat shirt, cover and tennis shoes. Some of us made the mistake of putting our "cover" on and were told in no uncertain terms that we were never to wear a cover inside a building unless we were "under arms," wearing a cartridge belt; nor were we ever to be outside without a cover on. We were told to pack the rest of our new clothing into our sea bag and we formed up outside in the rain.

Sergeant Hunt, who hadn't calmed down a bit, gave us

"Left Face," and we marched down the dark wet street. He called out the cadence, and anyone that got out of step, became the target of his special attention.

The shock of the last three or four hours was complete. I didn't know where we were going and didn't care. He could have been marching us into the fires of hell, and I was only concerned about keeping step.

We marched down the wet narrow streets between small Quonset huts and eventually were given the order, "Platoon Halt, Right Face." We were told to break ranks and get our "sorry asses" in the huts. The hut was furnished with enough bunks to sleep about twenty recruits. I picked a top bunk in the middle of the right row of bunks and stood at attention while the DI roughly informed us of what was expected of us. After awhile, he gave us the order to undress to our boxer shorts and stand at attention by our bunks (racks). At the order, "Ready, Mount!" we jumped into our racks and lay at attention. He then ordered, "Ready, pray!" followed fifteen seconds later by, "Ready, Sleep!" He shut off the lights and exited our hut.

I lay on my back, stared into the dark and tried to gather my thoughts.

"Good Grief! What have I done?" was the first thing I thought. Then I remembered my choices.

For as long as I can remember, I have always had a deep interest in history and the military. Upon graduation from my small country school, I planned to join the Army or Marines. The Vietnam War was full blown, and I wanted to be a part of it, and history. But I had a girl friend, Debbie, and I really wanted to be with her. Debbie and her parents insisted that I would never amount to anything unless I had a college degree. So, instead of joining the military on graduation in 1967, I enrolled the next fall at Northeastern Junior College in Sterling, Colorado, about twenty-five miles from my home.

My grades were a reflection of how much I hated college. Then, two weeks ago, Debbie fell in love with the shoe sales boy that had fitted her for some new shoes. I had no reason not to enlist. On February 29, Leap Year Day, 1968, I skipped classes (nothing new there), and rode with some friends to see the nearest recruiters in Greeley, about 90 miles away. My friends went to see the Army, Navy and Air Force guys; I went to the Marine recruiter.

Why the Marines? I recently looked at my high school yearbook. Many of my classmates that signed it mentioned my desire to join the Marines and go to Vietnam. It is obvious that my classmates conspired to subconsciously lead me to join the Marines.

The Marines had a two year, a three year and a four year enlistment. I asked about the rumor that if I joined for four years, I would be more likely to get the job I wanted. The Staff Sergeant sighed and asked if I wanted "Aviation Guarantee." I told him that I was thinking more along the lines of "Infantry." Stifling a laugh, he said I was more than likely going to get that anyway. I signed up for four years. If they would have had a twenty year enlistment, I would have signed that.

That night, I went home and told Mom and Dad what I had done. Dad said that because I had signed up on Leap

Year Day, I would be in for sixteen years. Dad always looked at things that way. *I always told him, "Dad, they say an optimist sees the glass as being half full, the pessimist says it is half empty, you would say 'probably poison.'"* He would laugh. He loved to laugh.

I made sure the word got out that I had joined the Marines, and Debbie decided that being my girlfriend was the patriotic thing to do. Debbie was always a patriot, and we became a thing again.

As I lay in my bunk trying to go to sleep, I remembered that I almost didn't make it here. On Monday, the fourth of March, only two days ago, Mom and Dad drove me to Denver for my physical. I passed with flying colors until they checked my hearing. The doctor told me that my hearing was too bad, and that I could not be accepted into the Marines. Fighting tears, I told him that I had a cold right now, and that it was very important that I join the Marines. He looked at me for a moment, and then, after a visible sigh, he shook his head and signed the paper allowing me to join.

Laying on the bunk starting into the dark, I smiled; everyone here seemed to speak loudly enough for me to hear them. In spite of the rude reception, this is where I wanted to be. I closed my eyes and fell asleep in the middle of my nightly prayer.

It seemed I had just gone to sleep when my dreams were shattered. The lights came on, and Sergeant Hunt and two more "Smokey Bear" Marines burst in the door banging on trash can lids and shouting. Shaking bunks, they screamed at us to hit the deck. We couldn't do it fast enough for them. As we stood at attention at the foot of our bunks, the other two Smokey Bears loudly introduced themselves as Senior Drill Instructor Staff Sergeant Hogrefe and Drill Instructor Staff Sergeant Gill. Our three DIs demonstrated how we were to make our racks (beds) and told us to do it. After we finished, we were to form up on the street outside. We had ten minutes to use the head (restroom) down the street and get our hut in order. We failed miserably. DI Hogrefe screamed through our screen door for us to get on the street. The bunks were not all made, and half of us were not fully dressed. In varying states of undress, we stood in formation in the dim glow of street lights while Staff Sergeant Hogrefe inspected the hut. Mixed with a long stream of loud profanity, we heard the crash of bunks being tipped over. A mattress flew out the door and landed in a rain puddle in front of us. I was hoping it wasn't mine. DI Hogrefe came running out of the hut. He sidestepped the mattress and screamed,

"YOU PIGS GET BACK IN THERE AND MAKE THOSE RACKS LIKE WE TAUGHT YOU! NOW!"

We ran back into the hut to remake our racks. It was hard to believe that one man could cause so much havoc in such a short time. We set to getting dressed, uprighting our bunks and remaking our beds. It took us two more inspections before we satisfied Senior DI Hogrefe.

Once the eighty recruits of Platoon 152 were in formation on the street, Sergeant Hunt taught us a number of physical exercises. In addition to pushups, situps and jumping jacks we were taught how to do the exercise they called "squat hoopys." Squat hoopys were a six count exercise. On the count of "one" the recruit dropped from attention to a squatting position, knees out and hands on the deck between them. On the count of "two," the private kicked his legs to the rear for the start of counts "three" and "four," a push-up. Five and six counts reversed the exercise and brought the recruit back to attention. When we did the exercise, either as a group exercise or as a personal or group punishment, we counted as loudly as we could, "One, two, three, four, five, six, One Sir!" thus, one squat hoopy. After at least an hour of PT, Physical Training, or more commonly referred to as "Physical Torture," we were ordered to "Attention." DI Staff Sergeant Gill ordered us, "Left Face, Forward, Haw!" We marched to the mess hall and were taught the maneuver: "Form for chow."

In single file, we went into the mess hall doorway. We were instructed not to speak but only to put our steel tray forward if we wanted a certain helping of food. I side stepped down the cafeteria style counter. I put my tray forward, and a recruit in his fourth week of Boot Camp, put a large spoonful of runny scrambled eggs in one of the compartments. I put my tray forward for three pieces of half-raw bacon and a small stack of undercooked pancakes. At the end of the line, a recruit put a carton of milk on my tray. I followed the line to a table for twenty. We stood at attention until the table was full, and then the DI approached the head of the table and ordered, "Ready, Sit!" We sat at "attention" until we heard the order, "Ready, Pray!"

Only after the order of "Ready, Eat!" did I look down at my now cold breakfast. I wished I hadn't put my tray forward so often. My stomach turned. We had been instructed to, "Take all you want, but eat all you take." I was trying to wash down my cold doughy pancakes with warm milk when the DI decided we had had enough time to eat. He approached our table and screamed at us to get back on the street. We were marched to our huts and told we had ten minutes to, "Sh*t, Shower and Shave."

The restroom, hereafter referred to as "the head," was at the end of the street and had a maximum capacity of thirty or forty people. With eighty people crowding each other, it was less than a relaxing time. DI Hunt stuck his head in the door and screamed that time was up and get back on the street. After we were at attention on the street, the DI inspected the head. We had left a mess, and Sergeant Hunt was not pleased. He ordered us all on our hands and knees to clean up our mess. We vowed that the next time we would try to be a little neater.

The rest of the day was spent doing PT and learning the fundamentals of close order drill.

As we learned more of what was expected of us, each day was slightly better than the day before. We learned that if we got up a half hour before the DI came in, we could make our racks as well as we could in the dark, and put the finishing touches on them after the lights came on.

We were issued our M-14 rifles and learned everything about them. We took them apart and put them back together so often that we could do it in the dark. We were taught the:

"RIFLEMAN'S CREED"

"This is my rifle. There are many like it, but this one is mine. It is my life. I must master it as I must master my life. Without me my rifle is useless. Without my rifle, I am useless. I must fire my rifle true. I must shoot straighter than the enemy who is trying to kill me. I must shoot him before he shoots me. I will. My rifle and I know that what counts in war is not the rounds we fire, the noise of our burst, or the smoke we make. We know that it is the hits that count. We will hit.

"My rifle is human, even as I am human, because it is my life. Thus, I will learn it as a brother. I will learn its weaknesses, its strengths, its parts, it accessories, its sights and its barrel. I will keep my rifle clean and ready, even as I am clean and ready. We will become part of each other.

"Before God I swear this creed. My rifle and I are the defenders of my country. We are the masters of our enemy. We are the saviors of my life.

"So be it, until victory is America's and there is no enemy."

The rifle was a key ingredient in our close order drill. The "Manual of Arms" combined with marching was an everyday exercise for hours. The sound of an M-14 rifle falling on the pavement was never good news. A considerable amount of our daily PT also included the rifle. As a special punishment for messing up in drill, we had to hold the ten pound weapon straight out at arms length for longer than we possibly could. Anyone who let his arms fall less than parallel to the deck (the ground or floor) was the recipient of the DI's prompt attention. The six count exercise, "Squat Hoopys," were also a favorite punishment of the Drill Instructors. Drill Instructor Staff Sergeant Gill told us during a particularly hard PT drill, "It is only a matter of mind over matter people. I don't mind and you don't matter."

I think that every platoon had its own "Gomer Pyle," a recruit that just could not do anything right. I was grateful that I did not have that distinction. Private Clark earned the "Gomer Pyle" award.

One morning, after we had made our racks, we were all in formation in the street, all with the exception of Private Clark. DI Gill sang out in almost a sweet voice,

"Private Clark, where are you?"

Private Clark, bareheaded and barefoot, ran out of the hut and shouted,

"SIR, PRIVATE CLARK CAN'T FIND HIS BOOTS, SIR!"

In a very calm voice, DI Gill asked,

"Did you look under your rack, Private Clark?"

Private Clark ran back into the hut and emerged a few seconds later, still bareheaded but with boots in hand,

"SIR, I FOUND MY BOOTS! THEY WERE UNDER MY BED ALL THE TIME!"

I was trying to determine the expected punishment Private Clark was going to get. Once, I had not polished my boots to a DI's satisfaction and was ordered,

"Private Leis, squat hoopys, twenty repetitions, ready go!"

DI Gill stood looking at Private Clark,

"Private Clark, squat hoopys." He paused as he thought of the appropriate number, "forever, ready go!"

Poor Private Clark dug a hole in the sand about a foot deep before the DI let him stop.

In addition to PT and close order drill everyday, we also had classes on everything from rules, Marine history and regulations to weapons and hand-to-hand combat.

Platoon 152 was one of four platoons in the series. The series had all started boot camp at the same time and competed against each other. One day, we had bayonet drill against one of the other platoons. We formed a thirty by thirty foot hollow square. We were on one side of the square, and the other platoon was on the other side. We were fitted with football helmets and armed with a rifle-sized stick with cushioned ends. The man up would enter the ring to meet his opponent. The two would jab and parry with their sticks. It was not enough to knock the other guy down. If the standing man didn't "finish" off the downed guy, he got in a heap of trouble. The bayonet instructor acted as a referee and when one man had been "killed," the instructor would blow his whistle and declare a victor. The two recruits would then exit the pen and surrender their sticks to the next guys in line. The atmosphere was much like one would expect at a high school football game, and both platoons cheered their sides on.

The "Conditioning Course" was a series of obstacles to be overcome in as short a time as possible. It consisted of stuff to climb over, stuff to crawl under and stuff to wade through. I enjoyed the course. There were also Endurance tests, Combat Readiness tests and Physical Readiness tests, none of which I disliked. If I disliked something about boot camp or the Marine Corps in general, it would be the inspections. I didn't mind the rifle inspections or even the uniform inspections. What I really hated was the "junk on the bunk" inspections. Everything the Marine Corps had issued you had to be arranged on your rack (bed) exactly by the book. All folded just so. *My wife will attest to my inability to fold clothes "just so."*

We were marched to the head two or three times a day to relieve ourselves. On occasion, that was not enough for some. One day, while standing in line for mess, Private Clark decided that he couldn't wait. He broke ranks and ran up to DI Hunt,

"SIR! PRIVATE CLARK REQUESTS PERMISSION TO SPEAK TO THE DRILL INSTRUCTOR, SIR!"

"Speak."

"SIR, PRIVATE CLARK REQUESTS PERMISSION TO MAKE AN EMERGENCY HEAD CALL, SIR!"

DI Hunt asked him,

"What do you hear when there is an emergency Private Clark?'

Private Clark answered that he didn't know.

The DI told him,

"I want to hear a siren all the way to the head (several blocks away) and back, Private Clark. Go!"

Suppressing a smile, I heard Private Clark's version of a siren fade as he ran to the head, then grow in volume a minute later as he ran back to the platoon. The hardest time I had in boot camp was keeping a straight face. An ill-timed smile in life is bad. An ill-timed smile in boot camp could, and likely would, result in physical pain.

One day, we were a little lax while eating lunch and were talking quietly amongst ourselves. The DI heard us and told us that we could no longer use forks at mess until we "got our sh*t together." We were told, in no uncertain terms, that we were not Marines. We were the lowest thing on earth, "Right below whale sh*t, and that's at the bottom of the ocean." We were not allowed to blouse our trousers (tuck the bottom of our trousers under an elastic band on the top of our boots). Our shirts were buttoned up to the collar.

On the forth week of boot camp, I served a week in the DI's mess hall. My duties were like those of a waiter, except I never got a tip. I stood at "Parade Rest" where I could see all of my assigned tables. Whenever a DI, or group of DIs were ready to order off of the menu, one would shout "Smedley!" I had no idea what that meant, but that is what they called me, and when they called me, I ran over to their table, snapped to attention and took their food orders by memory, no paper and pencil. One day, a DI ordered "hot tea with cream." In my small world before the Corps, I had never heard of anyone drinking "tea with cream," so I assumed that he meant "coffee with cream." I got in trouble for that assumption.

With the exception of Sunday, we had mail call at the end of every day. We sat on the street as the DI went through the mail and called out the name on the next letter. Upon hearing our name, we jumped up and ran to the DI and snapped to attention and reported, ie,

"SIR, PRIVATE LEIS, SIR!" *"Leis" is a German name pronounced as "Lease."*

The DI held the letter out, and we slapped it between our hands to take it from him. This was a procedure so the DI could determine if something other than paper was inside the envelope. We had been instructed to inform everyone that wrote to us that we were not to receive anything other than paper.

One day, an unfortunate Private received a bulky letter. The DI had him open the letter, and it contained a pack of Juicy Fruit gum. The Drill Instructor asked the Private if he had enough for everyone, alas, five sticks of gum for eighty people. I was sure that the guy would spend the rest of mail call doing squat hoopys. We were all surprised when the DI told the scared recruit that he could eat the gum, but he had to eat it all right now. "That guy got off easy," I thought. The recruit started to open the pack of gum when Sergeant Hunt interrupted him,

"Uh uh, I did not say unwrap it."

The poor Private had to eat the unwrapped package of Juicy Fruit gum, paper, foil and all.

The week after the "gum thing," during some down time, the call came down the huts, "PRIVATE LEIS TO DUTY HUT!" Oh no! I never saw anyone that liked that summons. I ran to the Drill Instructor's Duty Hut, knocked three times loudly and reported,

"SIR, PRIVATE LEIS REPORTING AS ORDERED, SIR!"

Staff Sergeant Gill was on duty and yelled at me,

"GET IN HERE!"

I removed my cover as I stepped inside and stood at attention.

"Why the hell are you getting packages, Private Leis?"

"SIR, THE PRIVATE DOESN'T KNOW, SIR!"

He handed me a thin 3x5 inch package and asked who it was from. I looked at the return address and told the Drill Instructor that it was from my Aunt and Uncle. He told me to open the package, which revealed a new wallet. As I handed it to DI Gill, I thought, "Man, I hope I don't have to eat this." He looked at it and asked, "What the hell you gonna do with a wallet?" I was very lucky that Staff Sergeant Gill was on duty and not either one of the other DIs. It wasn't that Staff Sergeant Gill wasn't strict, he just didn't enjoy it as much at the other two. He gave me my wallet, told me that I better not get any more packages and dismissed me. That night, I wrote to Mom and told her to let everyone know to never send me anything other than paper.

After every mail call, the DI would ask how many of us received "Dear John" letters. Almost everyday, a few more hands would go up. My hand went up on about the third or fourth week. Debbie really liked those shoes. By this time, I half expected it, and I now had more pressing problems. *It was not to be my last "Dear John" from Debbie.*

We were never allowed away from the Platoon. Once every two weeks, we were marched to the PX, the Post Exchange. The DIs told us what we could buy: soap, razor blades, toothpaste and cigarettes. I was grateful that I didn't have a nicotine habit because we were only allowed to smoke when the DI gave the order, "The Smoking Lamp is lit for one cigarette. Do it." To which we were taught to reply as loudly as we could, "SIR, THE LAMP IS LIT FOR ONE CIGARETTE. SIR, WARNING: SMOKING MAY BE HAZARDOUS TO YOUR HEALTH. SIR, MARINES DON'T LIVE LONG ENOUGH TO DIE FROM CANCER ANYWAY! SIR!"

By the fifth week, we had, for the most part, learned how to avoid the DI's wrath. Drill was becoming something almost enjoyable. We had been taught to slam our heels down on the deck as we marched and to slap the rifle as loud as we could during the manual of arms. There is something quite exciting about hearing eighty people marching as one. After we had mastered marching and the manual of arms while marching, one of the D.I.s became imaginative in his drill. Drill Instructor Sergeant Hunt taught us the "Tea Berry Shuffle Maneuver. At the order "Tea Berry Shuffle, Ho!" we learned to do a little shuffle dance in the midst of our marching. After we had mastered, it he would show off our new maneuver to other drill instructors. Under the DI's ever vigilant eyes, mistakes became rare. After a particularly good day of drill, they gave us our forks back. We felt as though we had won an award.

One day we were told to fall in without our utility jackets, and we marched to the dispensary. We were to receive our immunizations. The line went in one door of a little building and exited out a door on the other side. We formed up according to how our last name fell in the alphabet, (A's first in line, Z's last in line). Leis put me pretty much in the middle. Before I entered the first door, the recruits whose names started with A, B and C were coming out the other door and were forming back up. Blood was running down some arms from having flinched while getting the shot from the immunization gun. The bloody guys hammed it up for our benefit. I removed my cover as I walked through the door, and two Corpsmen on either side gave me a shot in each arm. I followed the line down a corridor of Corpsmen toward the exit door. Each Corpsman was armed with either an immunization gun or a stack of syringes. We seldom got sick while in the Corps.

Every platoon had a guide. It was a position of honor as he carried the platoon Colors, a flag pole with a foot and a half square red flag with yellow fringe. Our platoon number was sewn in yellow on one side with USMC sewn on the other. Whenever we won a competition (drill, physical fitness tests, etc.) with the other platoons of the series, we received a streamer to put on the top of the flag pole. There was always a strong competitive spirit between the DIs of the four platoons of the series. If we placed badly in a competition, we could count on our Drill Instructors being a little rougher. The Platoon Guide marched at the head of the platoon, and upon graduation from boot camp, was to be promoted to Private First Class and receive a set of Dress Blues.

Our guide was a tall, muscular, good-looking guy whose father was a minister. He was like most of the other preacher's kids I knew when I was growing up, just a little "holier than thou" kinda guy. The DIs razzed him a lot about his religion, and by the fifth week of boot camp, he was smoking and cussing with the best.

Every Sunday, we were marched to church. The DIs told us, "Your heart may belong to Jesus, but your ass belongs to the Marine Corps." Once we were marched to the base theater to see a movie. I don't remember the sermons or the movie. Whenever we had the chance, we slept, and the church and theater both presented such an opportunity.

On about the sixth week of boot camp, we were loaded onto green Marine Corps buses and driven to Camp Pendleton to qualify with the rifle. We spent a couple of days "snapping in" and learning how to shoot the "Marine Corps Way." After three days of live fire practice, we shot to qualify. There are four possibilities in qualifying: Expert (the best), Sharpshooter, Marksman and failure to qualify. Because of my background on the ranch, I had spend many hours shooting. I knew I would qualify and hoped to make "Expert." I was only a few points short and instead qualified as "Sharpshooter." I was not too disappointed because I felt the Sharpshooter badge, a Maltese cross, was cooler looking then the Expert badge, crossed rifles. *"Cool" was very important at that age.*

When we came home to our huts in San Diego, we were given permission to "blouse our trousers" and unbutton the collar on our utility shirts. Although we still were not allowed to call ourselves "Marines," we at least looked like Marines.

Boot Camp normally took twelve weeks. It was shortened to nine weeks when I went through. The DIs told us, "They're in a hurry for little green amphibious fu*ks in Vietnam."

On May 13th, 1968, 69 days after the yellow footprints, we fell out in our dress summer uniforms and marched to the large base parade ground. Accompanied by a Marine Corps Band, we marched with the other three platoons of the series around the parade field and passed in review before a stand. We stood at attention in front of the stand while speeches were made. Some members of the graduating platoons had family members that made the trip to San Diego for the ceremony and were seated on bleachers behind the stand. At the end of the speeches, we were pronounced to be "Marines" and were dismissed. We threw our covers in the air and congratulated each other.

That evening, the last I had in San Diego, Sergeant Hunt read off the Military Occupation Specialty (MOS) of everyone. This was critical. When we first arrived in Boot Camp, we filled out a questionnaire asking about our education and skills we had before joining the Corps. I wrote down that I had experience with large machinery (farm tractors, trucks, combines, etc.) because I was hoping for a MOS in armor (tanks) or infantry. I neglected to check that I had two years of typing in school because I did not want to be a clerk. Most of the platoon were 0300, Infantry. My name was called, and Sergeant Hunt told me I was a 2531 MOS, field radio operator. I was surprised. I almost didn't get into the Marines because of my hearing. It would not be the last time I wondered about Marine Corps logic.

Chapter 2
ITR, LEAVE, RADIO SCHOOL & STAGING

After boot camp, we were bussed to Camp Pendleton, California.

We went to the INFANTRY TRAINING REGIMENT (ITR). Every Marine had to go through that training. It was less mental than boot camp but very physically challenging. We went on lots of long, hot and dusty marches with many nights camped under the stars. The amount of dust was in proportion to how far back in the column one happened to be. I was always somewhere in the middle, not the best place, but certainly not the worst. We started out with "March," which was done in cadence. Cadence ended when the troop leader gave the order, "Route Step, Ho!" Everyone just tried to keep up with the pace of the troop leader. We were carrying a rifle, helmet, a large backpack and water. The troop leader was only in his utilities, was healthy as a horse and could move almost as fast. The column became spread out, and the dust picked up another notch. After an extended "route march," people fell out and dropped to the side of the trail. Other troop leaders were following the column to "encourage" those who dropped out. An ambulance followed for those who fell from heat exhaustion or injury. Camp Pendleton is a big place, and I saw more of it on foot than I desired. We also had a lot of weapon training, becoming familiar with the various infantry weapons the Marine Corps used.

One of the troop leaders was a short Corporal whose name I cannot recall. He was a Vietnam veteran and one of the troop leaders in charge of our training. The troop leaders were only slightly easier than D.I.s, and this Corporal was a good story teller. He came into our hut (wooden building where 30 Marines slept), and someone shouted, "Attention!" He gave us, "As you were," and we continued what we were doing. I was polishing my boots and sat back down on my foot locker to continue my task. The Corporal jumped up on a foot locker in the center isle and started one of his silly lectures. He was a funny guy, and because I didn't think he could see me, I let down my guard and smiled. Remember what I said about an ill timed smile. He screamed,

"WHAT ARE YOU SMILING AT, PRIVATE?"

Oh no, I thought, some poor sucker was caught smiling.

"YOU LEIS, WHAT ARE YOU SMILING AT?"

Oh no, I am the poor sucker.

He called me to attention and proceeded to yell in my face. I was not too concerned. I figured it was a sticks and stones thing. He decided that yelling in my face was not sufficient punishment for "smiling." He ordered me,

"Get on your wall locker, Leis."

I had no idea what I was supposed to do with that order and just stood there dumbfounded.

"You don't know what getting on your wall locker is, do you?"

His voice and anger level rose,

"EVERYONE, UP ON YOUR WALL LOCKER! NOW!"

None of us knew what to do. Some guys just stood there, and some were trying to climb to the top of their wall lockers. He stopped us and explained that, "up on your wall locker" meant that the private was supposed to hang by his upper arms on the wall locker with his legs bent at a 90 degree angle parallel to the deck. So, we all got up on our wall lockers while he chewed us out for 15 minutes. Then he gave the order to get down. I jumped down, and he said, "Not you Leis, get back up there." And I hung there for another 15 minutes while he told us more crazy stories.

It really did not hurt. But after he left, I noticed that I could not pick up anything with my right hand. My left hand was weak, but my right one was dead. I had pinched a nerve and had no strength in my right hand, and I had to ask for help to tie my boots. The next day, we were to fire the M-14 rifle full automatic. When my turn came and the instructor told me to fire, I did not have enough strength to pull the trigger. He became annoyed that I wasn't firing and asked me why. I explained that I had pinched a nerve, but I believed that I could pull the trigger with my left hand. He said, "Oh no, if you can't pull the trigger with that hand, you can't hold it down either." So that day, I didn't shoot. Over the course of the next few days, the strength in my hand gradually returned.

For some unknown reason, I seemed to draw trouble in ITR. There was a duty called "Fire Watch Duty" that rotated through the unit. Fire Watch involved wearing a helmet, a cartridge belt and carrying a night stick. The Fire

Watch man was to patrol the whole area of huts and see that there were no unauthorized things going on, or a fire. I drew that duty one Sunday afternoon.

Halfway into my four hour shift, I walked through my own hut. As I walked through, I noticed that everyone had their name-stamp-kit out and were in the process of stamping some new article of web gear we had been issued. The Private First Class in charge of our hut told me to get out my stamp-kit and stamp that piece of web gear. I replied that I would, just as soon as my Fire Watch Duty ended. Harshly, he informed me that he was in charge, and he was ordering me to stamp said web gear now. OK, I thought, it shouldn't take but a minute or two. In the middle of the process, one of the Troop Leaders (the guys really in charge) walked in and caught me in the process of "neglecting my assigned duty." "This can't be good," I thought.

And it wasn't. He ordered me to follow him to the Troop Leader's Hut. There he informed the other troop leader on duty that this private thought that doing personal stuff was more important than his "assigned duty." They had me stand at attention against a wall. One grabbed my helmet and one grabbed my night stick and tried to wrestle them away. "I am never to surrender my weapon" came to me from some class, and I resisted as well as I could. But one finally won and took my helmet. I figured that the game was over and surrendered my night stick. Then, as I stood at attention against the wall, they took turns bouncing my helmet and my night stick off my head. Not hitting me, just bouncing them off my head. They did not ask why I chose to neglect my assigned duty. Excuses are not accepted in the Marines. The only acceptable excuse is, "The Private's mistake!" They continued to lecture me about the importance of following orders, while all the time bouncing my helmet and night stick off my head. Then they asked me if I understood. I replied in a loud, "Yes, Troop Leader!" I was given back my helmet and nightstick, and I resumed my "assigned duty." After that, my hut leader lost any respect he may have held in the hut. He had not come forward and confessed that he had given the order to stamp that piece of web gear. I, on the other hand, gained a few friends because I didn't snitch. For just a little pain, I earned a few friends and learned a lesson, a bargain anytime.

On July 13, 1968, the day after my 19th birthday, during the morning formation, a number of us were promoted to Private First Class. I was among them. I now had one stripe.

The dreaded gas day was upon us. We had all heard the scuttlebutt about the gas chamber, and secretly, if not openly, feared it. We were marched to a little cinderblock building in the middle of nowhere that looked all too much like the photos of WW2 German gas chambers. We were ordered to take out our gasmasks and were given a short lecture on how to use them. Then we were informed of what we were going to do inside that little cinderblock building. We were going in, twenty at a time, wearing the mask. Once everyone was in and the door was closed, we were going to get the order to take the gasmask off, and we would all sing "The Marine Corps Hymn." We could not start singing until the last guy had his mask off. Then, we would put on our gasmasks and come out. Simple.

I was with the third group of twenty to go in. I could see by the reaction of the first and second groups that came out that it may not be that simple. As soon as the door opened, the tear-gassed Marines came scrambling out of the fog, falling over each other in their desperate search for air. Most were vomiting and all were spread out as if to claim "this area of oxygen."

My group marched into the building wearing our gasmasks. The walls on the inside looked like the walls on the outside. The dim lights in the ceiling were covered with what looked like the old mason jars my Mom used to can fruit. The fog of gas blurred everything. People in gasmasks have always appeared a little scary to me, and this was a very scary scene. We were jammed in so tight that if I had fainted, which didn't seem out of the realm of possibility, I wouldn't have fallen down. The instructor waited until the door was closed; then through his gasmask, gave the order to remove our gasmasks. Always the obedient Marine, I followed orders and immediately removed my mask. Unfortunately, not everyone was as obedient as me. "We can't start until everyone has their mask off," the Instructor said through his mask. I tried to hold my breath, which probably did not help any, because when I finally gasped, I got a lung full of gas. I really do not know how long we were in there. I do know that we did not sing "The Marine Corps Hymn." We mostly gagged and coughed. I have seldom in my life felt sheer panic. The time I spent in the gas chamber was one of those times. When the door opened, our group was no more dignified than the previous two groups had been.

After we graduated from ITR, we were granted two weeks leave. I flew home to Colorado, and Mom and Dad picked me up in Denver. I do not remember very much about that leave. My great aunt passed away while I was home, and I wore my dress blues to that sad occasion. Mom gave a picnic for me and all of my old high school buddies. I felt like I didn't belong with them anymore. I went to see Debbie's folks. Debbie was in school in Mexico, so I did not see her. Her parents and I had a nice visit. Girl's parents always liked me more than the girls themselves, it seemed. While home, I dated four different girls I went to high school with. Much to my dismay at the time, all the girls were very nice girls.

Maybe the high point of that leave was when Dad put on his old WW2 Army uniform. Dad was a skinny guy, and his uniform fit him the same as the day he was discharged. We posed in our uniforms for the 8mm movie camera and did a few facing maneuvers together: right face, left face, about face. *It is a very special old movie.* That night, after everyone else was asleep, Dad and I sat at the kitchen table over a cup of coffee and talked about his experiences in the Army during WW2. I knew he had been wounded on Okinawa, but try as I might, I never could get him to tell me much more than that. He answered all of my questions that night and told me much more than I had known before. He told me that it was not like the movies, that bad things happen, don't stick my head up and never volunteer for anything. It was the most serious I had ever seen him unless I was in trouble for something.

All in all, I was very glad when leave was over and I could get back to doing what I felt I should be doing. Parting was, for my family, a sad occasion. I would not be home again until after Vietnam. Many of my extended family members had made the 100 mile trip to see me off.

I learned years later from my cousin, Craig, who was five at the time, that after I got on the airplane, all the women were in tears and the men were not far behind. Craig told me that he could remember that he realized this occasion must be something big. I was surprised that anyone had cared that much. Although there was always love in our home, tears were somewhat rare unless there was a wuppin' involved. It was a rare event to see the wuppers cry.

My flight took me back to San Diego, which, as it turns out, is quite a distance from Camp Pendleton. It seemed that if I took a bus, I was going to be late. I remembered the lectures about being late. If I took a taxi, I could just make it; that is, if I had the money to take a taxi. So I accepted the fact that I was going to report late, 8:00 pm as opposed to 7:00 pm. Maybe no one would notice. As soon as I reported to the duty NCO (non-commissioned officer), he took me and two other guys that were late into the Duty Officer's room. We were chewed out and threatened with all kinds of bad things. But the lieutenant let us go with a stern lecture. *That experience must have had an effect, because that is the last time I can remember being late to anything. In 32 years of punching the clock at the Post Office, I was never late one day. I didn't go in at all some days, but I was never late.*

The next few weeks were a happy time with few duties. I was assigned to a large modern barracks. By now, many members of my old boot camp platoon were going different ways. People that have the same fate tend to desire each other's company. In this case, all the guys with the same MOS started to hang with each other. We were all going to be field radio operators, so we would be together for at least awhile. One of my good friends, Johnny Wallen, was from West Virginia. He was a couple of years older than me, so I considered him wise. He was a great guitar and banjo picker. He went to camp services where he checked out a guitar and played and sang for me for hours. We got a three day pass one weekend and hitchhiked to nearby Oceanside. Three of us, Johnny Wallen, Ron Vlietstra and I, hitchhiked into town and rented a room. Johnny was old enough, so he bought a bunch of booze, and for the first time in my life, I got drunk, sick drunk. *I still don't understand why I would ever do that again.*

The next day we walked downtown to a music store that had banjos. Johnny asked and was allowed to try one out. The store owner came out and asked Johnny if he would like a job teaching, but Johnny couldn't take the job; Vietnam was only a few weeks away.

After a week of doing nothing, I was assigned to mess duty for two weeks. This time, I was not serving D.I.s. I was assigned to the "spud locker" to a private who was on his second week of mess duty. He was the "Spud Locker Honcho." He taught me the responsibilities of that esteemed position. We peeled thousands of potatoes and broke thousands of eggs into 30-gallon stainless steel pots. The second week, I was the "Spud Locker Honcho." It was my first position of responsibility in the Marine Corps, and the spud locker became a fun place.

My new guy, Bill Kramer, was a big good natured fella from an Ohio farm. He was a talented singer, and although I am not, he insisted that I join him and sing all the old tunes while we peeled potatoes and broke eggs. When we were not singing, we would talk about girls and how they could break your heart and about what fate might await us. Marines call a good sit down visit for hours "B.S. (bull sh*t) sessions." There would be hundreds more B.S. sessions.

We enjoyed the egg breaking races the most. We started with an empty 30-gallon pot and cases of eggs divided between us. The trash cans were strategically located to receive the shells. Eggs on the right, pot between our legs and trash cans on the left. Seated on chairs on opposite sides of the pot, we started the race. At "GO!" we each grabbed four eggs out of the cases, two in each hand, went to the pot, broke the egg shells on both sides of the pot, dumped and discarded the shells to the left; all done in a matter of seconds. The first one to finish his cases of eggs won. Of course, every now and then, we had to have a "time out" because the pot was full, or because one of us dropped a whole egg in. We rolled up our sleeves and went in, looking for a whole egg in 20 gallons of what was going to be scrambled eggs. Sometimes we found it. *I am sure I still possess that amazing skill; however, my wife insists that I not try.*

We were sent to our various schools to train in our MOS. MOS # 0311 (infantry) continued on into advanced infantry training. Those of us with a 2531 MOS went to radio school. We went to classes on radios and radio procedure. We did a lot of field work and lugged the 25 lb. PRC-25 field pack radios up a mountain called Sheep Sh*t. We learned how to clean them and maintain them. We had two weeks of radio training. That was enough to learn, as we said, "Push to talk, release to listen." On the 13th of August, I graduated from the BASIC FIELD RADIO OPERATOR SCHOOL.

A few days later, we were marched to a big building with hundreds of other Marines. We stood in line to get our individual orders. We all expected that we would be sent to various units in Vietnam, and most of us were right. This is the Marine Corps, and from the very start, we knew when we signed up, we signed up for Vietnam. A few didn't get orders to Vietnam. I saw some of those few actually shed tears of disappointment.

We lined up in front of tables arranged by MOS. I stood in line at the field radio operator table and waited for my turn. I took my turn, and a Lance Corporal seated behind the table picked up one of scores of stamps and stamped my orders. I read my orders and the imprint said:

"SU#1, 1st ANGLICO, FMF, WESTPAC"

OK, I knew FMF meant FLEET MARINE FORCE, and WESTPAC meant WESTERN PACIFIC (Vietnam), but I had never seen or heard of SU#1, 1st ANGLICO. I asked the Lance Corporal what Anglico was. He looked at the orders and said that he had no idea. He tapped the Corporal working beside him, showed him my orders, and asked him where I was going. The Corporal shook his head and said he had never heard of it. The Lance Corporal gave me back my orders, looked into my eyes and said, "You're going to hell, private." That made me a bit anxious. Luckily, one of the guys I went through boot camp with, John Staunton, also had the same orders; so if I was going to hell, I wasn't going alone.

From there, all those with Vietnam orders went to staging, the final training before we went to Vietnam. This training was short and dealt mainly with what to watch for in the way of booby traps, ambushes and how to search a village. One day, we drew our M-16 rifles. We went down a line, and a Marine read off the serial number of the rifle as another Marine wrote down to whom the rifle was issued. I received my rifle and was goofing and showing off to my buddies who were still in line. Ron Vlietstra turned to Johnny Wallen and said, "I just got this feeling. I don't think Leis is coming back." When Johnny told me what Ron had said, I laughed, but was internally unsettled.

A few nights after we finished Staging, Marine Corps buses took an airplane load of us to the airport in Los Angeles. We were all in a big room, laughing, joking and singing. In addition to the "Marine Corps Hymn," we sang every popular song we could think of. The atmosphere was much like a party.

I stood in line for a long time in front of a pay phone to make two calls, one to my parents and the other to Debbie. I should have skipped the second. It left me feeling empty. I regretted that I had talked to her and hurried back to join my buddies. We laughed, joked and sang all night until we got on the plane.

The commercial jet was much quieter than the airport. As we lifted off, we all turned to watch the lights of California and the United States dimming in the night. Not a word was spoken. All eyes watched, even after the lights had disappeared. Then, as if a silent order had been issued, we turned forward in our seats and closed our eyes, each of us in our own thoughts. Into the unending darkness we flew. I said a silent prayer. Next stop, Okinawa.

At Stapleton International Airport when I came home for my first leave. (left to right) Mike, Me, Mom, Dad, (in front) Jeff and Dan.

With My Grandpa and Grandma.

With my Dad, one of my favorite photos.

Johnny Wallen and Ron Vlietstra

Chapter 3
Good Morning Vietnam

The darkness did end. It was morning when we landed in Okinawa. I had been raised in Colorado, and I had never been further east than Nebraska. I went to boot camp in California. In short, I had only been in dry climates. When I stepped out of the door of that plane, I was hit with something I had never experienced, extreme humidity with extreme heat. Not as hard to breathe as in the gas chamber, but a sound second place. "So," I thought to myself, "this is the place where Dad had been wounded." I eventually adjusted to the climate, and thanked God that I was not stationed here.

The Marine Corps was using the base at Okinawa as a staging point for Vietnam. We stayed there for just a few days, during which we packed and stored all but one of our stateside uniforms. We were issued our new tropical gear: jungle shirts and trousers, jungle boots, ponchos, poncho liners, salt tablets, iodine tablets (to purify our water before we drank it), anti-malaria tablets and the rubber lady (air mattress). It was late night and raining before we finished, formed a column on the street and started back to our temporary quarters.

There was something quite melancholy about being in a column of Vietnam bound Marines; trudging sea bags down a wet dim street with only the tapping of the rain on ponchos calling a gentle cadence.

We also received a new round of shots, including the

worst shot I had ever had. I rolled up my sleeve, and the corpsman told me to drop my trousers. This shot was supposed to help the blood coagulate faster if we were wounded. A good thing, I guess, but that shot hurt for days. Two days after we had arrived in Okinawa, we left for Vietnam.

At 10:10 am, August 31, 1968, 179 days since the yellow footprints, I flew into DaNang. Just as every eye had been focused on the lights of the United States disappearing that night, all were now on this place called "Nam." It was very green and beautiful, but pockmarked with bomb craters everywhere. We could see explosions in the distance. We were informed by Marines who had been here before that they were probably air strikes. Those returning, experienced Marines were a prized source of information. We all wanted the real scoop from a real veteran and sought their knowledge.

We landed and went into a big receiving hangar where we reported. There were Marines seated behind tables, and they made arrangements to send the "Fuc*in'A*s NewGuys," pronounced "FANGs," to their assigned units. DaNang was in the Marine Corps' area of operations, so most did not have to go very far to reach their units. Johnny Wallen and I said goodbye. John Staunton, the guy I had been with since boot camp, and I stuck together because we both had ANGLICO orders. We gave our orders to a Marine seated behind a table, and he, like everyone else it seemed, had never heard of ANGLICO and had no idea where to send us. Finally, someone figured out that ANGLICO was part of MACV (MILITARY ASSISTANCE COMMAND VIETNAM, pronounced "Mac V") and that Headquarters was in Saigon. At 1930 (7:30 pm), we caught a C-47 cargo plane going to Saigon. The cargo plane did not have seats, and we sat on the floor. The hydraulics were exposed, and the banging, whining and whooshing made me somewhat anxious. We were now in Vietnam. Like a nervous cat, every new sound put me on alert. Fortunately, it was not a very long trip.

We landed in Saigon at night, and someone from the airport called Anglico HQ, and they sent a jeep for us. John and I checked in with the duty NCO about midnight. They gave us a rack, and we slept. The next day, we were issued our M-16s and learned about ANGLICO.

ANGLICO is the military acronym for "Air Naval Gunfire Liaison Company." Anglico had people with every allied military in Vietnam, except the U.S.M.C. John and I were told that we were going to the 2nd Republic of Korea Marine Corps Brigade (BLUE DRAGON BRIGADE), about twenty miles south of DaNang. Providing the Koreans with air strikes, naval gunfire, medivacs, and helicopter resupply required the largest contingent of Anglico people. Ninety Anglico personnel were assigned to this Korean brigade. The Anglico clerks told us they had to do some processing that was going to take a few days; after the morning formation and policing of the area (picking up cigarette butts), we could come and go as we pleased.

John and I needed someone who had as much experience as possible to hang out with. So we became acquainted with a somewhat boisterous Private Tom. He looked, talked and acted as if he knew the ropes and where to go and what to do. So, with another new guy named Conner, we followed him. The four of us went downtown into Saigon that morning. *I cannot remember if everyone was allowed to go into Saigon. Sometimes, because we were with MACV, we were allowed to go to places others could not.* Tom knew exactly where to go and how to get there. The Viet Cong had attacked Saigon during the '68 TET OFFENSIVE and had controlled some of it for a short time. We were armed with our M-16s, and John, Conner and I were a little nervous. We rode around on rickshaws in the insane traffic, walked the streets, smelled the smells and ate the food. As the day went on and we didn't get shot at, or shoot at anyone, we became less nervous. Tom decided we just had to go visit this little "skivvy house" he frequented. We didn't think that was something we wanted to do. Tom insisted that we go and that we didn't have to do anything. For that reason, and because he was going, and we had no idea how to get back to base, we agreed.

We followed him down an alley to an unmarked door. He knocked, "rap…rap…rap.rap.rap…rap." An eyeball appeared in a little hole of the door. Shortly thereafter, the door opened. We followed a Vietnamese girl into a dimly lit, smoky 10 foot by 25 foot room. The sweet smell of incense and what I assumed to be marijuana was almost overwhelming. There was a bar on the right long side of the room with chairs on the opposite side. As we walked down the aisle between the bar and the chairs, we could see a bright red curtain straight ahead. That led into another area where I could only imagine what transpired. John, Conner and I took chairs in the middle of the line of empty chairs. I made certain that my chair was not the closest occupied chair to that curtain. Tom went up to the bar and started visiting with the girl bartender. After a short time, a young, cute girl in a skimpy dress came out from behind the curtain and sat in the chair next to me. In very good English, she asked me my name. I thought there was nothing that violated my upbringing by giving someone your name, so I told her.

She asked,

"Cott, you want beer?"

I was a very inexperienced drinker, and I thought I might need all my faculties today.

"No, thank you."

She paused,

"You want happy cigarette?"

If a beer would mess up my faculties, I could not imagine what that would do, and answered,

"No, thank you."

John and Conner were snickering at my discomfort loudly enough for me to hear them.

She asked,

"You want boom boom?"

By now Conner was laughing out loud. I sat back in my chair and pointed to him,

"No," I told her, "but he does!"

With that, she jumped up, grabbed Conner's hand and they disappeared behind the curtain. I was still congratulating myself for having gotten out of that "dangerous" situation when Conner walked through the curtain wearing a goofy smile. We left shortly after that and made our way back to base. Conner was not sure if he was mad at me or not. I had never had so many new and different experiences in one day. Interesting day, I thought to myself. We learned later that Tom had been in country for a total of one week.

For the rest of our time in Saigon, John and I stayed on base. We did go to the enlisted man's club. It was a very nice club with live entertainment consisting of an all Vietnamese rock band. They played and sang the popular American songs with only a hint of a Vietnamese accent. Half of the many young Vietnamese girls were waitresses. The other half, provocatively dressed and highly perfumed, roamed the floor and asked servicemen to buy them drinks at exorbitant prices. As long as the drinks (tea) kept coming, she would stay and pretend that she thought you were interesting. The more the tea flowed, the friendlier she would become. But as soon as the drinks quit, she would abandon her patron in search of another. I believe that one of the requirements for a girl to get this job was to have a bladder the size of a basketball. Many lonely guys believed the high price of tea was worth the female company. For the most part, the girls had the luxury of choosing their victims, at least for awhile.

Saigon and the large area around it was in the U.S. Army's zone of operations. And thus, other than the Embassy guards, ANGLICO HQ staff, and us, there were no other Marines in Saigon that I knew of. This base employed a large contingent of hired Vietnamese help. While staying there, I had been surprised a few times in the head by the cleaning lady coming in and doing her work. She was fully involved in her work and could care less if the room was busy. I thought, "Well, this is different."

John and I went to the airport at noon, Sept. 9th, and we boarded a C-47 bound for Da Nang. This one had web seats strung up to the walls for passengers. Like a cat that has gotten used to a noise, I was more comfortable on my trip back to Da Nang.

We landed at Da Nang mid-afternoon. We got off and asked someone how to get to the Korean Marines. He probably had never heard of ANGLICO, but he knew about the Korean Marines. He pointed to a UH-34D helicopter, an old helicopter that looked like a grasshopper, and said it was going our way in a few minutes. Maybe we could catch a ride. We ran over and asked the pilot, and he said he had room. We hopped on and had a seat. All the crew (pilot, co-pilot and one door gunner with a mounted M-60 machine gun), had headphones and could communicate with each other over the substantial noise.

We took off and headed down the beach feet wet; "feet wet," I learned, is "radio talk" for "over water." Maybe I had read too many LIFE magazine stories, but I really expected we were going to shoot at someone and probably get shot at. So I locked and loaded my M-16 so I could help the door gunner. Turned out, the door gunner not only did not want my help, but was concerned that some stupid FANG would shoot us down. I gathered he meant me, so I unloaded my weapon and sat back down.

In about 30 minutes, we landed at a sandy base. The landing pad itself was constructed of slabs of perforated steel fastened together to make as large a landing pad as required.

It was still dusty, but better than nothing. John and I jumped off on landing, and ran, bent over off the pad, while shielding our eyes from the dust as the helicopter took off. We were greeted by a Marine who directed us, "up the road half a mile and the building is on your left." Still trudging our sea bags, we walked up the dusty road made worse by the heavy military traffic.

After we reported in, we were assigned racks in one of the huts, a wooden building with screening on the top half of the sides to allow for air circulation. There were about 10 racks to a building. The permanent residents had claimed a small area around each rack. There was 24 hour electricity at this base, and every permanent resident had a fan and a light on his footlocker. There was a much more casual attitude here than at any other quarters I had stayed in. The individual areas were decorated with photos and pinup calendars with days crossed out. There were a few guys playing cards and a few others writing letters as we walked in. We stashed our gear and started to check out our new assignment. One of the card players got up after the hand, came over and introduced himself as Freddie. Freddie then introduced everyone else in the hut, and all were very friendly. We wanted information, and they were all eager to fill in the FANGs. We were here to support the Koreans.

The Blue Dragon Brigade was responsible for eleven miles of coast along the South China Sea, approximately fifteen miles in depth. Within the Brigade, there were four infantry battalions, an artillery battalion and a ranger company. Each of the infantry battalions had 10-12 Anglicomen. At battalion level, there were three infantry companies plus a heavy weapons company. Each of the infantry companies were assigned two Anglicomen. Those not assigned to a company maintained a 24 hour radio watch at battalion. Unless there was something going on, the companies only had to check in at appointed times. In my opinion, life at Brigade H.Q. would be safer, have real hot food, a little club, the beach about 100 yards away, 24 hr. electricity, and would be tedious. I was hoping I would be assigned to a battalion and then a company. That's why I joined. *And to think my parents worried.* After we had run out of questions, we sat down with a group and learned new card games. *We played a lot of cards over there.*

That evening, I had my first contact with a Korean Marine. A Korean private knocked on the door of our hut and asked if he could come in. He spoke English well enough that we could understand that he wanted to make a trade. Freddie stepped up and started to negotiate with the Korean private. The Korean wanted to trade uniforms at the rate of: one set of Korean Marine Corps (KMC) uniform for one set of USMC uniform.

During the ongoing haggling, I asked one of the other guys why we would trade. He explained that if I was assigned to a company in the field, it would be a good idea to just look like another Korean radio operator. He also told me that we were authorized to wear the Korean uniform. The Koreans wanted our uniform because they wanted a souvenir. One has to remember, there were only approximately 90 U.S. Marines to a Brigade of Koreans, thousands of people. In their eyes, we were considered someone good to know. That desire to be friends with the Anglicoman increased at company level. There, if a Korean was hurt, the guy that got him out was the Anglicoman. *Still, I found, you had to earn their trust.*

Freddie was a talented negotiator and soon had it to: two KMC uniforms for one USMC uniform. After haggling for another half hour, it was agreed that they would trade uniforms at a rate of: three KMC uniforms to one USMC. The KMC private then went around the circle of Anglico guys, shook our hands and told us we were, "Number one!" *Number one is the best grade a person or situation can get. Number ten is the worst grade.*

We were all feeling pretty good about being number one when Freddie decided that he didn't want to trade. We went from "number one" to "number f*ckin' ten" very quickly after that. We finally convinced Freddie that he should keep his part of the bargain, and we all became number one again. As I planned to go to a company, I took advantage of the negotiated deal and exchanged one of my uniforms. If I needed a U.S. uniform, all I had to do was request one. Freddie never did make it to "Number One." As the Korean left, he paused at the door and pointed at Freddie, "You not number one. You maybe number four."

I never had to stand radio watch at Brigade. On the morning of the 16th of September, John and I were sent out to 5th Battalion.

Brigade Anglico H.Q

Good Morning Vietnam

Chapter 4
5th Battalion

John and I packed our sea bags and waited on our racks for a ¾ ton pickup truck from 5th Battalion. A bespectacled skinny corporal walked in and announced that he was the team chief of 5th Battalion's Anglico team. He explained that 5th Battalion was on a Battalion size operation right now and that some of their Anglicomen were about to rotate back to the United States, including himself. They had replaced one, but one of us was going to have to go out to 26th Company in the field right now. I cannot say why he picked John as opposed to me. It didn't look like he gave it a lot of thought. We were going to drop John off at a helicopter pad, and from there, he would be flown out to 26th Company in the field. We would take his sea bag back to the Battalion Permanent Command Post (C.P.). John would only take his combat equipment which consisted of:

Rifle, flak jacket, helmet, cartridge belt with k-bar and/or bayonet, at least 2 canteens of water and the first aid kit. We used the cloth bandoleers that ammunition came in to carry 20-round magazines, loaded with only 18 rounds each. We had heard that when you fully loaded the magazine that it put stress on the spring, and the magazine could fail to function. <u>Anything</u> that fails to function in a combat situation can be fatal. It may have only been a rumor, but why take the chance.

Once in the field, John had to share the responsiblity of carrying and operating the 25lb. AN/PRC-25 radio (prick twenty-five) with his counter-part. There would be up to five smoke grenades hanging on the straps holding the radio to the pack-frame. The pack-frame also had an accessory bag with a 10 foot sectional whip antenna in its own little plastic bag, cleaning tools and maybe an extra handset. We normally used the three foot tape antenna unless we had to use the 10 foot one to maintain radio contact. A spare battery in a plastic sealed bag was strapped to the bottom of the radio. The black plastic handset had a hook that allowed it to hang on the breast pocket of the flak jacket. To top off the look, there might be a hand grenade or two hanging somewhere.

The equipment that an individual Anglicoman might take to the field varied greatly between one man and the next, as well as from one operation to the next.

John and I jumped into the cab of the truck with Corporal Willis, and he drove north out of the compound. After three miles of driving through a scattered forest, we came to a branch of the road. We stayed on the main road as it curved to the west while the branch continued north. Pointing to the branch, Corporal Willis yelled over the rough road noise, "That's the way to 5th Battalion C.P." He added, "But only the one guy getting ready to go home is there right now, name's Jim Marshal." He explained that all the Battalion C.P. Anglico personnel were also in the field at a "Battalion Forward" C.P. After three or four miles of a more rolling open and rough terrain, we passed a small rough trail on the right that disappeared in the brush and rolling hills. I thought I detected a shudder as the Corporal said, "That's the trail to 27th Company." After a couple of miles, we came to a very large and busy LZ (Landing Zone). We pulled in and parked.

"This," the Corporal explained, "is the Korean's main

supply base. Everything comes into here and is distributed as needed. This is also where the large troop lifts into the field originate." Indeed, there were twin-rotored CH-46 cargo helicopters and trucks coming and going the whole time. Some of the helicopters were hovering over large nets full of boxes of ammo, k-rats (the Korean version of our c-rations) and large metal tubes containing water. Korean ground personnel fastened the nets onto the hovering CH-46 and then hurried away as the helicopter, with a blast of wind, lifted off with the cargo. The whole operation was a very well choreographed dance between man and machine.

The LZ was called LZ DUSTY because of the Corporal that ran the American side of the show. Dusty, I learned, had been at that position for almost three years. He had continued to voluntarily extend his time in Vietnam six months at a time. *I found that if you had been in country for 18 months, to someone in country for 18 months and one day, you were considered a FANG. Everyone I knew was a FANG to Dusty. He was very good at what he did and had been promoted a number of times. But Dusty did not respect the authority of some higher ranked people and was busted as often as he was promoted. Whatever his current rank was at the time did not affect the operation of LZ DUSTY. It was always extremely efficient.* Dusty was an affable guy, even to a FANG, and I enjoyed being around him. He knew when the next helicopter was going out to 26th Company and we left John to catch his ride. I hated to leave John. We had been together since boot camp and that felt like a long time. It seemed that all too often when you said "Good-bye," you never saw that person again. We were reassured by Corporal Willis that we would see a lot of each other in the future.

As we got back into the truck, Corporal Willis told

me that we had to go out to 27th Company to give the Anglico guy his mail, a case of c-rations and a carton of cigarettes. He did not seem to relish the idea. He stopped at the turnoff, buttoned up his flak jacket and fastened his helmet strap. He explained that a Korean truck had been ambushed on this trail yesterday and both the occupants died.

Uh oh, I thought as I followed his example. I locked and loaded and got ready for the trip. The road was very rough, and we could never go more than 10 mph. We had to ford a couple of flooded areas, the largest was a couple hundreds yards long. We drove past a burned and bullet ridden trunk that had been pushed to the side. It was while we were in the middle of the water that I most expected shots to ring out. It is hard to hug the ground in water. After what seemed like a long time, we topped a small hill, and we could see 27th Company about 1000 yards away on a little rise to the northwest. I breathed a sigh of relief when we were inside the wire.

27th Company CP looked like something out of a movie. It was a small square area, around a hundred yards (plus or minus) to a side. Surrounding the compound were three rows of perimeter concertina wire. Planted in front of the inside wire were claymore mines with interlocking fields of fire. *Claymore mines are command detonated anti-personnel mines that are used in defensive or ambush positions.* Every twenty-five yards or so, inside the wire, was a bunker with a .30 machine gun. *The U.S. Marines had the M-60, but the Koreans were still using the WWII model 30 caliber.* A double line of zigzagging sand bagged trenches connected all of the M.G. bunkers together. The Koreans had cleared an area around the position about 800 yards out to provide an excellent field of fire. Beyond that, there were scattered woods to the west, north and east with only small clumps of trees to the south. The open ground was a combination of rough, brushy ground, with large patches of six foot grass. The whole area was sprinkled with flooded bomb craters and low areas.

The compound itself was set up with a few sandy roads and full of small to medium sandbag bunkers. There was little movement inside the compound. Guards were in the M.G. bunkers, and here and there, a KMC was about, but most were staying out of the midday heat. Because 27th Company was on an operation, there was only a skeleton force left to defend the CP.

In addition to small arms, each Korean Company had 81mm mortars dug into pits within the compound. For further defense, they could call in "four deuce" (4.2 in) mortars at Battalion or artillery from the Artillery Battalion. And of course, the Anglicoman could bring air support in the form of helicopter gunships and/or air strikes. At night, we could summon a "Spooky"/"Puff the magic Dragon" gunship. Reinforcements could be heli-lifted in if necessary.

We pulled up beside one of those small bunkers, and Corporal Willis shut off the truck. A tall American, wearing only a dark handlebar mustache and a pair of faded Korean camouflage trousers, came up from the bunker and leaned on my truck window. The Corporal introduced us, "Leis, this is Lewis, Lewis, Leis." We shook hands. Willis had told me Lewis was only a couple of months away from going home. He would normally be back at Battalion, but because 27th Company was on an operation, he had to come out here. *Before I left, I served with all three companies of the*

Battalion. *All saw their share of rough operations, but only 27th Company C.P. was this exposed to attack.* The sand was hot, and Lewis was hopping up and down in his bare feet. He asked us to go inside the bunker.

Willis had told me that the Anglicomen at 27th Company C.P. had the worst living conditions of any of the companies in 5th Battalion. The best thing that can be said about the Anglicoman bunker is that it was a small target. The bunker was an 8X6 foot hole in the ground. Sand taken from the hole filled the two-layer green nylon sandbags which had been used to build the four foot high walls of the bunker. The wooden roof was covered with three layers of sandbags. Behind a sandbag blast-wall, there were a couple of steps made out of wooden ammo boxes going down to a homemade screen door. I got the c-rats from the back of the truck and followed them as they ducked to go into the 5 ½ foot tall interior. Inside, there were two cots separated by a table. I put the c-rats in the only open corner and sat down on the left cot by Willis, opposite Lewis.

As my eyes adjusted to the dim light, I could see the walls were plywood and had the usual decorations, pinups, family and girlfriend photos and always the calendar with days crossed off. The flies were really bad, and a flyswatter lay on the cot next to where Lewis had been reading a paperback western. It was noticeably cooler inside the bunker. Willis put Lewis' mail and a carton of Marlboro cigarettes on the table. Lewis had his flyswatter and was targeting a fly's' LZ. After the kill, he opened the carton of cigarettes, lit one, and picked up his mail.

While they were talking, I looked around. Neatly arranged on the homemade wooden table were a couple of candles, a dark green plastic canteen, a lantern and a green military flashlight. Lewis had been writing letters, and his writing kit was out. There were two used c-rat cans. The two inch tall "B-1 UNIT CRACKERS AND CANDY" can had been converted into an ashtray, which was in use right now. The other, also a two inch high can, "B-2 UNIT CRACKERS BEVERAGE POWDER," had been modified into a heat tablet stove. On a shelf above the table was a canteen cup, a dozen paperbacks and a worn deck of cards. Lewis' prick 25 radio, rifle and helmet were at the foot of his cot on top of a foot locker. His green camouflage poncho liner served as a bedspread. A dark green wool blanket lay folded on the foot of his cot. His flak jacket was his pillow. Lewis was only here until the operation was over, in about a week. Then the 27th Company Anglicomen would come home and enjoy all these comforts.

Their conversation caught my attention. I heard Lewis telling Corporal Willis how badly he wanted to go back to Battalion. It was also his opinion that the new guy, tilting his head towards me, could relieve him. I tried hard not to show panic. Frankly, Lewis' situation here scared the bejabbers out of me. He was isolated here with a skeleton force of KMCs. For all I knew, 1000 V.C. might be hiding in those woods to the north, just waiting for me to be alone! I did not know the first thing about calling in air support, medivacs or reinforcements. This place looked like one or all of those skills might be crucial. Thankfully, Corporal Willis was as aware of that fact as I was, and explained to Lewis that I did not have enough experience. Lewis grudgingly agreed, and I tried to hide my relief. I was still gung ho and wanted to go to a company; just not by myself right now. To drop me off there would be like dropping me off on the moon. I wouldn't have a clue what to do next.

Lewis hated to see us leave, but Corporal Willis was anxious to get going. He had to drop me off at Battalion Rear, and then he had to go out to Battalion Forward in the field. We bade Lewis farewell and buttoned up our field jackets, strapped down our helmets and locked and loaded for the trip out to the main road. It was as uneventful, but no less tense, than the trip in had been. After we hit the main road, we turned east until we reached the north branch we had passed earlier. We headed north along a road that was only slightly better than 27th Company's trail. There were woods on both sides of the trail. I could tell by Corporal Willis' demeanor that the danger level had dropped significantly. We drove past the burned out ruins of a stone Buddhist temple on the right. As I stared at the temple, I caught glimpses through the trees of waves crashing. Midway between the main road and 5th Battalion C.P., we drove past 25th Company's C.P. on the left with the usual wire and bunkers. We topped a little rise and drove past Korean guards who waved us through the gate of 5th Battalion's Command Post.

The base was much more substantial than the companies; much larger, more wire, more claymores, bigger bunkers and more of them. It looked like they were here to stay. On the interior of the defenses were wooden huts scattered among sandbag bunkers. Here and there were small clumps of trees. Willis had to stop and shift into four-wheel drive because of the deep sand. He pointed to the right. In the sparse woods was a large and substantial bunker with many radio antennas. "That is the TOC, Tactical Operations Center." We drove around a curve to the east and through an open area. This large sandy area was 5th Battalion's parade ground. The parade ground was bordered on the north by the

Korean Mess Hall, on the west by a stage facing the sea and on the south by the Anglico Bunker/hooch. Fifty yards to the east of our hut, just beyond a single wire and a couple of machine gun bunkers, lay a beautiful sandy beach. As I looked at those cooling waters and listened to the waves, I thought of Lewis. I understood why he argued his case so hard.

As we drove up, a tall lanky guy, dressed in shorts and a sleeveless green t-shirt, came out of the hut. The hut (sometimes "hooch") was wooden but was protected all around by sandbag walls. Willis introduced me to Jim Marshall, and we unloaded John and my sea bags. Corporal Willis grabbed a couple of fresh radio batteries and a case of c-rations and left for Battalion forward.

I followed Jim inside and paused to let my eyes adjust. I found myself in the northwest corner of a square 15 x 15 foot room. There were a couple of homemade wooden beds and a couple of cots. In the middle of the room was a 3x4 foot wooden table. A small American flag adorned the south wall, and there were photos, and as always, calendars. One thing about being in Vietnam, you always knew what day it was. In the right corner there was a tall homemade wooden chair that looked like a rough throne. In the far corner was a large homemade desk with two large shelves full of paperbacks and board games. Three or four folded lawn chairs and a square folding table were leaning on the wall by the desk. Directly across from the door where we entered was another door exiting out the sea side. To the right of that door was a homemade wooden shelf that held a metal five gallon water cooler. To the left of where I stood, there was an opening in a half wall to a 6x8 foot area with a cot. The half wall separating the small room and large room supported a 2x6 foot plywood countertop. An electric hot plate for cooking and a canteen cup holding eating utensils were on the counter.

Jim had been sweeping the plywood floor when we pulled up, and he picked up his broom to finish his job while we visited. Jim was one of the happiest people I had ever met. Happiness is contagious, and I enjoyed his company. Maybe part of his euphoria was that he was going home in about ten days. But I felt that he was always, and more importantly, would always be a happy person. We talked and visited the afternoon away, and then we had a c-ration dinner. Spaghetti and Ground Beef was my favorite at the time, and I heated two cans (that is <u>a lot</u> of spaghetti and ground beef!). Jim and I played a few games of cards. Then I wrote to all of my family, a few old high school friends, Debbie's mother, and all the girls I had dated, with the exception of Debbie, and told them my new address:

PFC George Scott Leis 2409915
Detach # 5 Sub# 1
1st Anglico, FMF 1st MAR DIV
FPO San Fran Calif.
96602

I loved writing "FREE" in the corner of the envelope where the postage stamp was normally affixed.

I blew up my rubber lady and lay down on one of the wooden beds to go to sleep. The next morning, I woke up on the hard surface of the wooden bed. My rubber lady did not last through one night of use before it went flat. It was just dawn when I woke up. Jim was not in his cot. I pulled on my trousers and went outside and heard someone singing, "It's a

Beautiful Morning." Jim was walking barefoot along the beach singing his heart out. The Korean guard in the bunker by the beach was laughing. Crazy American… But he was right, it was a beautiful morning. We still had the night's cool air. The sun was just rising over the South China Sea whose waves were gently lapping at the shore. The world seemed fresh and new. Jim was one of those rare people that recognized the simple and pure treasures in life.

That afternoon, we were joined by the man that John had been sent out to relieve. Jim introduced him as "Chief." Yeah, you guessed. Chief was a full blooded Native American. Chief was also rotating home soon and was all smiles. He joked that he hoped he was going home, but he was a little nervous about the American government and its history of treaties with the Indians.

Jim took me on a tour of the TOC. We left our bunker and followed a path west through the light woods. After about 20 yards, we walked by a three hole outhouse on the left. Not ours, ours was a two holer to the southeast of our hut. Ten yards later, we entered the TOC. As we walked down into the well lit bunker, Jim pointed to the right. Against the entry wall of the 10x10 foot area was a small, homemade table with a wooden chair. A Prick 25 attached to an external antenna wire was on the table, as well as two field telephones. One went down to our hooch and the other was a land line to Brigade. Above the table were a couple of shelves that held paper and pens. "That," Jim informed me, "is where we stand radio watch." It was the only radio in that part of the bunker.

To the left, the room opened up into a much larger 15 x 25 foot room. There was a line of Korean PRC-10 radio stations all along a narrow table that ran the length of the far wall of the bunker. *We had the PRC-25 radios while the Koreans were using the older model PRC-10s.* On the back wall, there were comfortable couches and chairs. Centered in front of the most comfortable chair was a slightly tilted 6 x 8 foot shadowbox table. A back lit aerial photo map covered the table. The map was covered with glass, and there were black grease pencil military symbols showing the positions of the different elements of the Battalion. Red arrows marked intended movements. Jim pointed out that that is where the Korean officers sat.

Because the Battalion HQ was in the field right now, very few of the radios were being manned here.

Jim introduced me to the Korean Lieutenant on duty. The Lieutenant was very pleasant and spoke English very well. He explained the map and pointed out the units and what they were doing. It was my first look at a map of the area. I studied it for a long time to familiarize myself. Jim explained that Anglicomen in the field had to know where they were at all times. "You can't call for someone to come and help if you don't know where you are." We had been taught map reading in Boot Camp, ITR and Radio School.

Jim instructed me on the procedure to follow in a medivac, resupply and air strike. 5th Battalion's call sign was "Scorcher One Four." The three companies were "Scorcher Alpha, Bravo and Charlie" (25th, 26th and 27th Companies respectively). All medivacs and air strike requests started with a call to Brigade, whose call sign was "Past One Four." Sometimes, if the company was operating beyond radio range, Battalion would relay the info to Brigade. Brigade would contact the requested support and send it to the company. We could talk to helicopters and most propeller-driven planes, but we could not talk with the jets. That required a UHF radio that was just too big and bulky to carry. If we needed an air strike, we would talk to a spotter plane. We would explain the target to the spotter and where all the friendlies were. He would then relay the info to the jets, usually a flight of two F-4s or two A-6s. The spotter would then tell us to pop a smoke grenade. We would pop a smoke, and the spotter plane would confirm the color. He would then fly over the target and throw a different color smoke out of the plane or fire white phosphorus rockets on the target to mark them for the jets. Then, get down. The ordnance was usually 250 lb. snake eye bombs or napalm. Snake eyes were dangerous and could throw shrapnel a long way. Napalm was very colorful and effective but could get very hot if you were too close to it.

Jim told me about the different priorities of medivacs. Emergency medivacs were WIAs (wounded in action) that were going to die or be maimed if they did not get to a hospital ASAP. Priority Medivacs were personnel that needed attention within a few hours. A priority medivac could become an emergency medivac if left too long. Routine medivacs were for slightly wounded people that needed medical attention but were in no danger of dying. Routine medivacs were also the priority used to evacuate the KIAs (killed in action). I asked about night medivacs when you could not use smoke to identify your position to the helicopter. He showed me the strobe light. It fit in my palm, and when I turned it on, it made a little whining noise followed by a bright flash. *Werrrr, FLASH Werrrr, FLASH*. He told me to always inform the helicopter when I turned on the strobe light. More than one strobe light had been fired upon by helicopters because the helicopter door gunner thought it was muzzle-flash, and they thought they were being shot at. Jim warned me that it was a dangerous job. Radio operators are always a priority target. Jim smiled. "A tall blond guy with a company of Koreans, with a radio antenna wippin' in the breeze, now there's a target." *We had heard from reliable sources that there was a price placed on Anglicomen heads.*

Jim also told me that while one of the two Anglicomen did the radio work, the other would find and search the LZ for booby traps; always a tense job. The bad guys knew where we would want to land a helicopter, and that fact demanded that the chosen open area be physically searched by the Anglicoman. That Anglicoman would also pop the smoke grenade or hold the strobe and guide the helicopter in.

A couple of days later, Chief taught me the art of "burning the sh.ter." A door on the back of the outhouse opened so one could pull out the two 55 gallon barrels that had been cut in half. The barrels were pulled away from the wooden structure, and the sh.ter burner poured diesel fuel in each half barrel and set them afire. The black smoke billowed into the sky. The burning barrels would then be replaced with previously burned ones. Thus, I learned the art of "burning the sh.ter."

It seemed as though something was always burning in Vietnam. A certain combination of burning stuff will flash me back faster than explosions.

The Koreans kept a generator on 24 hours a day for the TOC. Only during the evening hours between 7 pm (1900) and 10 pm (2000) would they run more generators and power the whole base. At Battalion, it was seldom absolutely quiet. There was always the hum of a diesel generator competing with the sound of the waves lapping on the beach.

The day or night would be quiet. Then in the distance, I could hear gunfire and explosions. If that fire was worrisome enough, we would go to the TOC and find out what was going on. We spent most of the time swimming and body surfing. The rubber lady air mattress made a great surf board for those whose rubber lady hadn't gone flat. For five days, this routine went on; no responsibilities, just eat, sleep and play. The war had forgotten me.

Since my rubber lady had gone flat, I had been sleeping on a cot. In the middle of one night, I was awakened by what felt like an earthquake, accompanied by a long continuous roar. The vibrations were so great it almost dumped me from my cot. And then, as suddenly as it had started, it stopped. I found my flashlight and turned it on. Through the settling dust, I looked at Jim. He turned on his cot to me. "Its OK, that was a B-52 strike." "Good grief!" I thought. I lay back down and tried to go back to sleep.

The operation ended and 5th Battalion came home. I met the Captain. *A Marine Corps or Navy pilot was assigned to Forward Observer duty with us. This duty rotated every 100 days and a new Marine or Navy lieutenant or captain would join us. We always developed a very good and professional relationship with those officers.* He only stopped by to pick up some clothes, and then he was on his way to DaNang to visit with his pilot buddies for a little RnR. Corporal Gettle, Lewis, Don, Marty, Scottie (Moses C. Scott) and Pete also came in when the operation ended.

A couple of days later, we took Jim Marshall and Corporal Willis into Brigade where they caught a helicopter going to DaNang, then a C-47 to Saigon. After a day or two of processing, they would then take a "freedom bird" back to the "world." I was going to miss Jim and was honored to have met him. We said goodbye. *And I never saw him again.*

I really enjoyed all of the guys in the Battalion. We became a tight knit group that enjoyed and appreciated each other. Corporal Gettle (we just called him "Gettle") took over as Team Chief when Corporal Willis went home. Counting Chief, there were five guys to maintain a 24 hr. radio watch. Each night, we rotated one man just up the road to 25th Company. Gettle let us decide how we wanted to run the radio watch. After some debate, we decided that an eight hour watch with twenty-four hours off sounded like a pretty good deal. We seldom had this many people. Radio watch was down in the TOC. We had to keep a log of everything that happened concerning us or one of our companies. Sometimes it got exciting, and sometimes it was a great time to write letters, learn card tricks and read.

One evening, I was making my c-rat "double can spaghetti and ground beef dinner with dehydrated onions." Don Webber walked in from his radio watch. He stopped and looked at my dinner, wrinkled his nose, and asked if I was going to eat all that. I replied that I was. He shook his head and said, "Anyone that can eat that much food and still be that thin has a tape worm. From now on, I am calling you 'Worm.'" It stuck. *Very few people were called by their first name. Many went by nicknames; I was one of those. I was called "Worm" and eventually became fond of it and wrote it in big black letters on the back of my flak jacket. Truthfully, I wish I had been playing cards when Don walked in; "Ace" would have been a nickname more to my liking.*

The Koreans had turned the power back on when they came in from the operation, and we now had electricity about 10 hours a day. That night, the talk centered on how great it would be to have one of those new real-to-real tape decks. Gettle said he wanted to buy one over here because it would be much cheaper and then take it home with him. It was decided that tomorrow morning, Gettle and I would hop on a helicopter and go to the PX in DaNang and get a tape deck and a speaker. Tomorrow night, we would have music in the bunker.

The next morning, Gettle and I hitched a ride to Brigade LZ and then hopped a helicopter going to DaNang. We found the Post Exchange and went tape deck shopping. Gettle bought a large Teak reel to reel, and I bought a Pioneer 88 speaker. We each bought a couple of tapes. Then, we lugged our stereo system until we found a helicopter willing and able to drop us off at home. Gettle had this hungry puppy dog look, and it seemed like his requests were never turned down. We were soon back at 5th Battalion with our stereo.

We all worked to get it set up. The speaker would not plug into the tape deck. After some discussion, we decided to read the manual. We found our problem. We needed something called an "amplifier." The next day, Pete was going to DaNang with the Captain, who had returned from his RnR. He picked up an amplifier for us. That night, we had music, not stereo music. A couple of days later, we figured out we were not hearing the whole song. *HEY! It was new technology*! I bought my second speaker the next time someone went to DaNang. *I still have and use those speakers.*

A week later, while listening to our new stereo, we decided that life would be just about perfect if we could get some food other than c-rations or Korean food. It was decided that tomorrow morning, Gettle and I would hop a helicopter going to DaNang. Instead of the P.X., this time we went to a mess hall. We were wearing our Korean camouflage uniforms which made us different than every other American, and I am sure that it helped our cause. Gettle told the Mess Sergeant that he was the team chief of 12 Marines that had eaten nothing but c-rats and Korean food for months. All true, but when Gettle told it, I almost started crying for us. They probably sent me with Gettle because I was skinny and looked hungry. The Mess Sergeant was very generous and gave us more boxes of stuff than we could carry. He also provided a truck and a man to take us and our food to the helicopter pad. We unloaded our stuff beside a large helicopter pad and thanked the driver. Gettle ran over to a running Huey and asked the pilot if he would drop us off at our battalion. He agreed, and the door gunner helped us load our goodies. There were boxes containing hamburger, chicken, buns, cake, soda and milk. We had a party that night.

While I was on radio watch a few days later, a company in another Battalion had a fire fight. The Anglicoman had called in three "priority" medivacs but could not get the helicopters because of the many "emergency" medivacs going on. It had been over an hour, and the Anglicoman said that the wounded Korean's friends were upset. They thought that it was the Anglicoman's fault that their friends had not been medivaced and locked and loaded their rifles on him. Finally, the helicopter came in, and we all breathed a little easier. I am sure that the offending Koreans were disciplined. I do not blame them for their actions, a buddy was hurt. I resolved to have good relations with whatever Company I joined.

One night, I was playing RISK with Gettle and Don when Pete, who was on radio watch, buzzed us on the land line. The Anglicoman that was with 25th Company, just up the road, called in, and he had a medivac. A Korean ambush team that was going out on ambush was receiving instructions on the claymore mine when someone accidentally set it off. The Anglicoman was a relatively new guy and was somewhat shaken by the carnage. Don Webber stood up and volunteered to go out there and run the medivac. I didn't. When Don came back after the medivac, he said it was a mess. I have always felt guilty for not volunteering to go with Don. I knew it was going to be ugly on a massive scale. I swore never to shirk my duty thereafter.

Everyone lived for mail call. It seemed as if our lives revolved around the mail. We had to go into Brigade to get our mail, so we only got it two or three times a week. I always had a very rewarding mail call. I was corresponding with my family and old high school girl and guy buddies. Debbie's mom, Jewell, had written to me and had even sent packages. Packages were always something very special. Most of the packages were food, which we shared with everyone. Some of it got damaged in transit. The addressee would shout, "Chocolate chip cookies, guys! Bring your spoons!" I got a letter from Debbie. It was a nice letter, and I replied likewise… Enough said.

The monsoons were upon us. It rained more than this

dry land farm kid had ever seen. *I like the rain. I like the mood it creates. The war pretty much shut down when the weather was that bad. So, maybe that is why I like rain.* Our hooch had many leaks. Sometimes a drip would turn into a trickle, and that could become a stream. Randy had a drip over his rack, so he tacked his poncho to the ceiling over his cot. That night, I was awakened by a large splash followed by a scream, followed by much bad language. We all flicked on our flashlights to see what the commotion was. Gettle lit the lantern. Randy's poncho had filled up with water until it could hold no more. As terrible as that was, it was pretty hard to keep from laughing. Well, maybe Randy didn't laugh as much as we did.

The rain seemed to go on nonstop for weeks. The Tactical Operations Center flooded. We ran a remote from the radio, which was attached to a large antenna in the TOC, to our bunker. We could send and receive, but we could not change frequencies. I was on the midnight to 0800 watch one rainy night when I had to change the frequency. Grabbing a flashlight, I ran to the TOC and stood on the step going down to the dark flooded room. I saw a stool and a chair floating by and pulled them to me. Then I leapfrogged using the two to traverse the ten feet to the radio. I changed the frequency without a problem, but in the dark, I had unknowingly pulled a wire loose. I leapfrogged to the door and ran back to the hooch.

Very quickly, I figured out what I had done. I ran back to the bunker. Sweeping the bunker with my flashlight beam, I searched for my chair and stool. I spotted them gently bobbing on the far end of the bunker. I removed my boots, socks and trousers to keep them dry and slowly walked down the steps. The water was cold. I waded through waist deep muck with crabs and other stuff I couldn't identify floating around. In my bare feet, I felt slimy things on the deck. That was about as bad as it got at Battalion.

In mid October, Don and I volunteered to relieve 27th Company Anglicomen so they could come into Battalion for awhile. The roads were flooded, and the exchange was delayed many times. Finally, during a small break in the rain, Gettle, Pete, Don and I climbed into "BANARD," the name we had christened our ¾ ton truck. Pete rode shotgun, and Don and I were in the back with all our gear. The trip was iffy from the start. The monsoons had flooded many areas that were high and dry before. We had to ford through flooded areas many times before we even got to the dreaded trail going out to 27th Company.

By now, 27th Company trail had become almost a "Sleepy Hollow" kind of place. The kind of place where boogie men hung out and you passed through carefully. After a slow and slippery, but otherwise uneventful trip, we made it into 27th Company C.P.

As we rolled to a stop, I thought, "These two guys are pretty excited," as they threw their bags in the back of Banard. They gave us a short briefing on the camp and its personnel as we stashed our gear. They answered any questions we had. Then, with a smile and a wave, they jumped in the back with their gear and Gettle started the truck. After getting stuck in the mud three or four times, they made it out of the compound.

The 27th Company guys had not improved their interior design skills. The bunker was as I remembered it. I took the left cot.

Anglico counterparts are, for the most part, very close. The monsoons started up again that night and it never stopped raining for days. Our bunker was on a little higher ground and never flooded. There are many people that I would not want to spend days with in a 6x8 foot area. I enjoyed learning about Don's life in California. He was a cool guy who had many fascinating stories. I don't know why, but he seemed to be interested in a farm and ranch kid and what farm kids did. He had a wonderful sense of humor and that was a priceless commodity. It is hard to be miserable when you're laughing. He told me a story about how he had a run-in with the police and how he had met a cute lady cop. She had been writing to Don and asked if he wanted anything. Don wrote back that he would like a .38 revolver. One day Don received his package from the lady cop. For some reason, that "Smith & Wesson" revolver and it's shoulder holster became the envy of 5th Battalion Anglico. I have heard, "A friend is someone who knows all about you, and likes you anyway." Don was a special friend, and I trusted that together we could do whatever we had to do.

When the rains stopped, the war picked back up. Almost every night the Koreans fired their mortars. Sometimes the sporadic fire would flare up with machine gun fire and flares. We stayed close to the Korean Captain in case he needed our services. I had my first medivac on one of those nights. One of the Korean ambush teams had a fire fight and they came back with wounded. They came to our bunker and woke us at 0100. Don had been in country for ten plus months and had done this many times. He had told me what we were going to do should this happen, so I did the LZ work, and Don was on the radio.

I had heard medivacs many times while on radio watch at Battalion. It was more intimate being on the scene. Don keyed the handset:

"Past One Four, this is Scorcher Charlie."

"Scorcher Charlie, this is Past."

"Roger Past, I have an emergency medivac."

"Roger that, standing by for zone brief."

"Zone Brief as follows: Our position is Zero, Seven, Four, Two *(four digit coordinates would get the helicopters close enough for us to guide them in on the radio)*. We have two Emergency KMC WIA. They were a part of an Ambush team that was in a firefight 1000 meters north. Last fire was taken one hour ago from same. The helicopters will be cleared to fire 300 meters beyond the perimeter of the compound. Best approach is from the south. Best departure is to the east."

Brigade requested the helicopters and we waited. Within 10 minutes, we spotted the blinking lights of two CH-46s approaching from the Northeast. The radio crackled alive with a warble all helicopter radios had. *You can recreate what the helicopter radio transmissions always sounded like by pinching and rapidly jiggling your throat while speaking their parts. I always wondered why the helicopter pilots did that.*

"Scorcher Charlie, this is Dustoff two nine."

Don answered,

"Roger Dustoff two nine, I am at your two o'clock 3000 meters."

The helicopters adjusted their flight path until Don told them he was at their twelve o'clock. When they flew directly overhead, Don would transmit to them "Mark Mark." Don then repeated the entire zone brief he had given to Brigade.

We had a small open area in the compound that we used as a LZ, so booby traps were not a problem. I stood in the middle of the open area, held the strobe light up at arms length, and waited for Don to yell "Strobe" before I turned it on. As the two helicopters flew over, Don yelled and I turned on the strobe light. Werrrr, FLASH. The helicopters saw the strobe and acknowledged it. The strobe was almost blinding, and I did not like holding that flashing light up in the dark any longer than I had to. One of the helicopters circled around to the south and started his approach while the other flew cover. *Werrrr, FLASH Werrrr, FLASH.* He came in fast on my strobe light and turned on his landing light in the last 75 feet. I tried to avoid looking at the light, and guided him in onto the small sand pit we called a LZ. He landed and I shielded myself as well as I could from the sand storm and watched as the Koreans loaded their wounded. I stepped to the side, and with an even bigger blast of wind, noise and sand, he was off and away. Kinda like stepping into a tornado for thirty seconds. *Werrrr, FLASH.* I shut off my strobe.

I had lost my night vision because of the landing light

and was reluctant to use my flash light. I tripped on something while walking back to the bunker. I turned on my flashlight for a second; it was one of the wounded Korean's bloody flak jackets. I stared at it for a moment. I thought, "He should be in the hospital in a few more minutes." I shut off the flashlight. I felt exhausted but satisfied. Night medivacs were always more intense. It had gone off without a hitch. Not all of them did.

Don and I stayed at 27th Co. C.P. until early November, and then we went back to Battalion. I stayed for a couple of days, and then I asked to be sent out to 26th Company. I told my Battalion buds goodbye. When I left, there was a bidding war going on for Don's revolver. Don was refusing all offers. Although I thought Webber's .38 was really cool, I didn't bid. I had a weapon; I didn't have a stereo system.

Gettle drove me to 26th Company's temporary home, the Ranger Company C.P., while the Rangers were in the field. The C.P. was just to the south of Brigade HQ, so it was a very secure area. I was excited to join my old buddy John with 26th Company.

Jim Marshal

5th Battalion

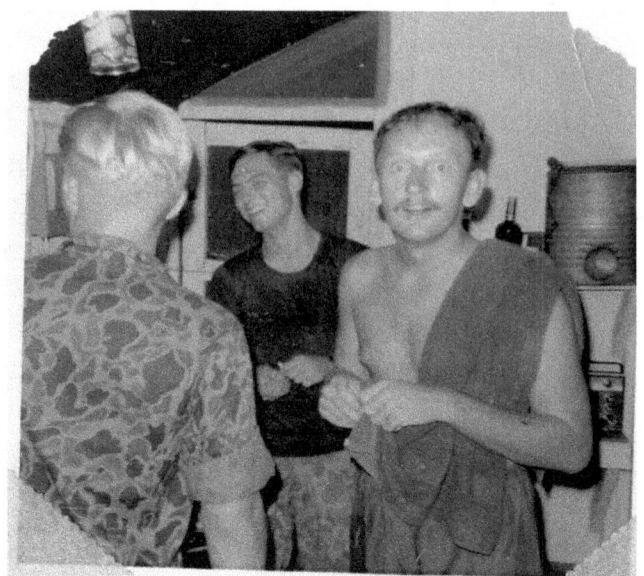

Marty, Don and Bill Gettle

Don fixing a snack at 27 Co.

Pete and Lewis

Chief, Marty and Randy (driving)

Trail to 5th Battalion C.P. during monsoons

Chapter 5
26th Company

John and the guy I was relieving, Mays, met us as we pulled in front of their hooch. The building was just like the ones at Brigade, except at Brigade, there were 10 Anglicomen per hooch and they had electricity. 26th Company had just come in yesterday from a two week operation, and John had saved his dark beard so we could see it. Some guys can really grow a beard. Mays was a good natured person with an easy smile. I always enjoyed his company whenever I saw him, but for some quirk of circumstances, we were seldom in company.

I have come to believe that when combined with one's decisions, "quirk of circumstance," to a great extent, dictates the course of a life.

We had brought John's two week accumulation of mail and parcels with us. John gathered up all his mail and I followed him into the hooch carrying two cases of c-rations. This was a pretty nice home. It was big. A big table sat between two racks (beds); much more comfortable than cots. John sat on a lawn chair, and after he glanced at the return address, he opened a box. His wife made some delicious chocolate chip cookies, and just as importantly, had packed them very well. It was always good when a buddy got a box from home. After John shaved, we sat, visited, drank instant coffee and ate cookies most of the day. He and I had been in the same Quonset hut in boot camp. He was the last link to my first days in the Corps.

John said that he thought 26th Company was a very

good company, and he knew the key people within the company. The most important person to us, in John's opinion, was Staff Sergeant Lee. Sergeant Lee was the Korean Supply Sergeant for 26th Co. He was a six foot tall skinny guy who was probably in his mid twenties. Sergeant Lee had been practicing his English with Mays and John, and had become quite proficient. John told me that we always took what we wanted out of our c-rations and gave the rest to Sergeant Lee's supply section cook. I asked John why we got so many c-rations. He said he wasn't sure, but he had heard that the two Anglicomen at a company were rated as a platoon of Marines, so we got a platoon's ration of c-rations. That seemed likely as we always had a lot of c-rats to give the Koreans. In return for the c-rations, we ate with the supply section.

With small variations, that meal was the same three times a day, every day. I came to love it. The course was always rice, kimchi and soup. The unwashed white rice came in large gunny sacks. I learned from the Koreans how to use the starch water from cleaning the rice to starch my cover (hat). It only took a few meals before I developed a taste for kimchi. I still love an occasional helping of that spicy and aromatic dish. My wife, and everybody else I know now, seems to dislike the strong smell of pickled fermented cabbage saturated in a highly spiced broth that has been buried in a pot for ten days. It's an acquired taste. The soup consisted of k-rations, (the Korean version of c-rations) our c-rations and whatever else the Koreans could find to harvest or kill. One day the soup was really good and I asked what the meat was. It was dog. I quit asking silly questions after that and just enjoyed the soup. I gained weight (no fat) while I was with the Koreans.

That night was my first meal with 26th Company, and I wanted to make a good impression. I never forgot the medivac when the Koreans locked and loaded on an Anglicoman. We sat cross-legged with Sergeant Lee on the sand, and watched a Korean private cooking our dinner. The rice was in an ammo can over an open fire. Sergeant Lee explained that the rubber seal had been taken out so that the can would not explode. A large kettle over the fire held the soup, which the cook would occasionally season to taste.

I told Sergeant Lee that I wanted to learn how to ask the cook for food in Korean. Sergeant Lee looked at me and asked, "You want to ask that man for food?" I answered that I did, and would he please teach me. He said something. I shook my head. Then he patiently taught me how to say, roughly: "Yama sao K asakee, bop E D wa?" I practiced until dinner was ready. Sergeant Lee was satisfied that I had mastered my "dinner question" and motioned for me to go use my new found language skill.

I took my mess tin to the cook, looked him in the eye, and asked very slowly, "Yama sao K asakee, bop E D wa?"

As it happened, I didn't ask him a question at all. I apparently said something about his mother, and he jumped up and started thumping his chest screaming "K asakee?" I swear he was almost foaming at the mouth. I backed off as he gestured wildly and aggressively with his ladle. The cook and I noticed Sergeant Lee and John rolling on the ground with laughter.

I realized that Sergeant Lee had taught me something quite different than "May I please have some food?" Still angry, but confused, the Korean cook stood with his raised ladle staring at Sergeant Lee. Sergeant Lee and John helped each other up, and then explained the joke to the cook who then had a good laugh. Moon, the cook, then came over to me and patted me on the back and gestured to the food. The story went around the supply section. I saw some of the KMC talking together, one pointed at me, and then they all laughed. I smiled. That's ok I thought, humor had always served me well. I had a great dinner.

*Thus, I learned my first Korean phrase: "Hello Son of a Bi*ch, give me rice!"*

John introduced me to the Korean Company Captain and officers. The Captain spoke no English, however his XO (Executive Officer), Lieutenant Kim, spoke excellent English. We talked most days with the officers because (1) we needed to know what the plan was, and (2) we wanted to strengthen our rapport with the company.

The Korean Marine Corps has the same pride as the United States Marine Corps, but they did things much differently sometimes. Corporal punishment was non-existent in the USMC after Boot Camp; unless you count a night stick and helmet being dropped on your head as corporal punishment. Not so in the KMC.

I had seen entire platoons in a position called "Kodabaca." The men were in line, and at the command, folded their hands on their head, bent over at the waist and fell forward with their head in their hands on the ground. Their bodies were formed in an inverted "V." The officer or NCO walked behind the line with a stick/bat and gave each man a hard wack just below the butt; sometimes sending the recipient sprawling. Speaking as a person that knows something about "whoopins," just below the butt hurts. It always bothered me to see that punishment.

I only saw Sergeant Lee use it once. The supply people had messed up in a way that made Sergeant Lee madder and more frustrated than I had ever seen him. After much ranting and raving, he finally gave the formation the order "Kodabaca!" John and I were watching from a short distance away. We knew most of the supply people, and had developed many friendships. It was hard to stand there as Sergeant Lee went down the line with his stick. He reached the end of the line and looked up. Our eyes met and I could see he was on the verge of tears. He turned away and dismissed his men as he walked to his bunker.

I had come to a few early opinions about the Korean Marine Corps. They were tough. They had a sense of humor. They made good spicy food. When I saw Sergeant Lee's eyes, I knew they were not without compassion. I liked the Koreans. I prayed for the strength, wisdom and courage to serve them well.

I have known many good officers and NCOs while I was in the Marines. This company had some of the best. Sergeant Lee loved his men like a hen loves her chicks. He watched out for them and was always fair. His men loved and respected him. When he was nervous or excited, he would rapidly blink his eyes. To me, he was like an older brother that talked funny.

John and I would often stay up half the night visiting, playing cards and listening to the radio. Many times we would not get out of the rack until late morning the next day. One morning we slept in, got up, ate, and then went back to sleep in the afternoon. Sergeant Lee came over that evening, and explained that this was his fifth trip over today, but we were always asleep. He was a little disgusted. "Why you all time sleep? Morning sleep, afternoon sleep. All time sleep!" I shrugged and explained, "Old American custom, Sergeant Lee." With downcast eyes, he shook his head. "I do not understand American custom."

He told us that he had come over to tell us that we were going out on an operation tomorrow morning. This was going to be my first operation. I didn't get much sleep that night as I thought about the upcoming day. It probably didn't help that I had "all time sleep" that day.

The next morning, we geared up and went to where the Koreans were boarding trucks. We always stayed with the headquarters group. After boarding the 6x6 trucks, we drove to a point a little further past and across from LZ DUSTY. We all disembarked, and a platoon started moving in a rough skirmish line across the rough ground to the south. I volunteered to carry the radio, and John held it as I put my arms through the straps. We followed the skirmish line in a spread out double column.

We started walking around 7 AM, and already the day promised to be a hot one. We had been moving for a couple of hours when I jumped at an explosion toward the front of our column. John turned to me and said, "Booby trap, come on." Sergeant Lee, John and I ran to the front of the column.

One Korean was dead. A badly wounded KMC was being attended to by the Korean corpsman. A couple of other slightly wounded were being bandaged by their comrades. The dead Korean had stepped on a booby trap which had almost blown off his right leg. The badly wounded Korean was walking too close and had multiple shrapnel wounds. The Korean Corpsman was pumping morphine in him to kill the pain. We had one emergency medivac and three routine medivacs. John told me he was going to search out a landing zone, and to "Go ahead and call it in."

I keyed the handset, and to my great surprise, I said nothing. After a moment of "dead air time," I released the "push to talk button" and took a deep breath. I paused. "Get it together, Scott," I whispered. I rehearsed what I was doing and started all over again. This time I had more success, "Past One Four, this is Scorcher Bravo." *I learned that it was of the utmost importance to be calm on the radio. Panic is contagious, and it must be kept under control. Helicopter pilots like to know that they are not flying into a panic situation. Panic was "number fu*kin ten." We all took great pride in how calm we could be in stressful situations.*

I carefully walked a short distance from the wounded over to the LZ John had picked out, and searched for booby traps. The helicopters came; I gave them a zone brief; John popped a yellow smoke, and it was over within a half hour from booby trap to medivac.

The company resumed its march. We had only been moving for ten minutes when another explosion, about 75 yards away, threw dirt and smoke up on a small hill to the left. John, Sergeant Lee and I ran to the hill. One of the flanking skirmishers had triggered another booby trap. Only one man was hurt, but he was badly wounded. As I started to call in my second medivac, there was a burst of small arms fire in a bushy area we had walked by 100 yards back. We got down and tried to figure out what was happening.

Brigade was asking for a zone brief and I had to tell them to "wait one."

The firing stopped, and we saw some KMC drag two black pajama clad figures out of the bush. It seemed like it was over, and I gave Past One Four my zone brief. As we waited on the hill for the helicopters, I could see that the prisoners had been taken to the Korean Captain, about 50 yards away, and were being interrogated.

I heard, and then I saw the two CH-46s approaching from the northeast. I was giving them the zone brief when a shot rang out. We hit the ground again and looked for the source of the gunfire. John was lying by me; he touched my arm and pointed down to where the prisoners were being interrogated. One of the black pajama clad figures lay sprawled on the ground. The other was gesturing with his arms, and we could hear his excited jabbering. I looked at John; he pressed his lips and shrugged to suggest, "that's the way it is." We stood, and I resumed my zone brief to the helicopters. After the medivac left, I asked Sergeant Lee about the prisoner. He told me the second prisoner had revealed where two SKS rifles and explosives were hidden. The Captain had been very mad at losing so many people. As we sat on a log, I asked John for a cigarette, and smoked for the first time in my life.

For those who are judging, war is a brutal experience and life becomes cheap. I hate the brutality of war, and there have never been wars without brutality. I am angry as I write this. I am not angry with the trigger man. I am angry with the people who put other people in that situation, then judge their conduct without experiencing their environment. Sergeant Lee and I had many conversations concerning the

Korean culture and background. The Company's fathers had fought a nasty Civil War against a brutal Communist enemy. Many had lost family members in that war, and they hated all Communists with a passion.

Shortly thereafter, we started moving again. I was very nervous, and stepped only in the footprints of Moon, who was walking twenty feet in front of me. Because my eyes were searching for footprints, I did not notice that Moon had stopped, and I almost bumped into him. We chatted a bit, and then he started walking again. He had taken three steps, when all of a sudden he fell as his foot dropped into a hole. I gasped and held my breath- But, no boom. I whispered "Jo con A!" which roughly means, "Oh my goodness!" I stared at the booby trap, and realized that I had almost been badly hurt. The booby trap Moon had stepped on had a grenade attached to a wire. By the grace of God, Moon had not triggered it. I helped Moon back to his feet. His eyes were big as he realized how close he had come to dying. I made sure I kept a decent interval between Moon and myself for the rest of the day. We had no more medivacs that day. After more persuasion, the prisoner revealed the location of more weapons and ammo.

We usually had two USMC amtracks (amphibious tractor), more often referred to as LVTs (landing vehicle tracked), with the company. Three or four guys made up the crew of each vehicle. There was a .30 machine gun mounted behind either a gun shield or a little sandbag bunker on top of the LVT. They carried a lot of the company's supplies, including stacks and stacks of bundled green nylon sandbags and entrenching tools.

Everything was a first time thing that day. When I

didn't know what to do, I followed John's lead. The column stopped. Sergeant Lee came back and told us this was home tonight. I was ready. The heat and stress of the day had worn me down. I followed John to where the LVTs had set up, and we introduced ourselves to the LVT guys. Because we almost always had LVTs with us, we got to know some of them pretty well. They would always find room for a few extras that we wanted them to carry out for us. Anglico guys and amtrack guys always got along great. We grabbed a couple of large bundles of sandbags and an entrenching tool.

We found out where the Captain's bunker was being built, and then we built ours close to his. We marked out a four foot by seven foot area. As we dug down into that area, we took turns holding and filling the sandbags. We built our four bunker walls with the full sandbags. When we took a break, I sat on our half finished bunker and looked around. Like an ant hill that has been kicked, the area crawled with busy life. Everywhere the Korean Company was busy building bunkers, gathering wood for cooking, unloading the LVTs and putting claymore mines around the perimeter. John picked up the entrenching tool, and I grabbed an empty sandbag. When we were done, the sandbag wall was about two feet high, and the hole on the inside was about the same depth. It was just wide enough for two rubber ladies to fit side by side. We had a little more room because only one of us had a rubber lady. We built a stick frame to suspend our mogie (mosquito) nets over us while we slept. For some reason, and for only this one time, we placed John's rubber lady at the back of the bunker with me by the door. Normally we both slept with our feet toward the door. Our rubber ponchos made the roof of our bunker. John blew up his rubber lady while I made fun of it.

Living With Dragons

We went over and visited with Sergeant Lee while supper was being made. Sergeant Lee's supply team had unloaded the company's ammo, water and k-rations from the LVTs and stacked it all nearby. In the late afternoon, the three of us sat down on a stack of those boxes and visited while we watched dinner being made.

John showed Sergeant Lee a photo of his sister, Carolyn. Sergeant Lee said she was very pretty. John asked him if he would like to write to Carolyn. Sergeant Lee started blinking his eyes rapidly. He said he would like that very much, but he could not. John asked why, and Sergeant Lee explained that he could not write English very well. John promised that he would help him, and Sergeant Lee said he would think about it.

I caught a whiff of the "soup of the night" and it smelled good. I always used one of the empty c-ration cardboard boxes as a rice bowl. Moon filled my box about halfway up with rice. He then poured a large spoonful of thick soup into my canteen cup. He gave me a k-ration can of kimchi and a little packet of k-rations spices. I then searched out a spot to eat. *Thinking about it makes my mouth water.*

After dinner, John, Sergeant Lee and I walked the position to familiarize ourselves with the situation. The badly bruised prisoner was blindfolded and restrained in a sitting position to a stack of k-ration boxes ten feet from our bunker. A KMC guard sat on a box opposite the POW. We had heard the prisoner screaming while we were eating dinner. We knew why when we saw that a field telephone was wired to him. *The field telephone has a crank that, when rapidly turned, sends a surge of electricity through two wires that make the phone on the other end buzz.*

Outside our bunker, we quietly visited with Sergeant Lee until it was almost dark. I made a radio check with Battalion for what we hoped was the last time until morning. We crawled into our mogie net tents. John lay down on his rubber lady, and I lay on my blanket over the ground. Our flak jackets were our pillows. We remained fully clothed and with our boots on. Our weapons and the radio were inside with us. We talked quietly for a little while before we went to sleep. We discussed how odd it was for two PFCs to be in this situation. We didn't think they were paying us enough. After we stopped, talking I thought of the day.

I had reached another conclusion about the Korean Marine Corps. In addition to what I had learned earlier, they were also ruthless with the enemy. I thought of my performance. With the exception of the first time I had keyed the mike and couldn't talk, I was satisfied. I had to find a way to not let the horrors of war affect my job. Part of that job was to talk calmly on the radio. I prayed I would find a way. As I drifted to sleep, I could hear the first drops of rain hitting the poncho.

I woke up to the roar of rain beating down. I reached above me in the dark and felt the bulging, water filled poncho only inches above my chest. I thought, "Oh no, if I don't get some of this water off, it is going to collapse." I slowly pushed up on the bulge, and I could hear the water running off. "Good," I thought, "only a little more and it should last till morning." All of a sudden I felt like I was getting wet from the ground up. I stopped pushing the poncho as the water came pouring in the door and washed away the foundation of the sandbags. The whole door side of the bunker collapsed, and the remaining water ran off the poncho and into the hole with John and me. I was laying in four inches of water. I turned and looked at John, expecting that he was really gonna be mad. But he slept on as his rubber lady gently rode the calming water. As the other three walls remained intact, he was now sleeping in a lean-to and remained dry. I was soaked to the bone. Everything I had was soaked, and it was still raining like the devil. I climbed out of the water, sat on one of the k-ration cases, and looked at my watch, 0145. I could make out the prisoner and his guard a few feet away. We sat there in silence till dawn. It was a long wet night. I found that it is one thing to get wet when you expect to get wet; it is a different thing altogether if you get wet when you expect to be dry.

The rain had stopped, and as the sun rose, the camp came to life. Smokey fires were started, and breakfast was being prepared. We had rice, kimchi and soup for breakfast. We asked the XO what the plan was. He replied that we would send out patrols, but the company was a blocking force, and we were not moving for four more days. Then we would be going in.

Typical tactic used was the "hammer/anvil" tactic. A hammer force (attacking) would push the enemy into the anvil (blocking) force where he would be destroyed. At least that is the way it was drawn up.

That morning, the Captain requested that we bring in a helicopter to take the prisoner out. As I waited for the helicopter, they drug the prisoner over and sat him on the ground. I glanced over at him. He was still blindfolded and was in rough shape. I tried to tell myself I didn't care, but I secretly prayed that the worst part of his ordeal was over.

John and I spent a good part of the day rebuilding our bunker and drying our stuff. Then I cleaned my rifle and wrote letters. When I made the morning radio check, I asked if we had any mail back there. Pete was on radio watch at Battalion, and he said we did have mail, and they would send it out on the next resupply. We were scheduled to get resupply the next morning.

That afternoon, one of the Korean patrols had contact, and we could hear the firing toward the southeast. The firing grew more intense, and the Captain decided to reinforce the patrol. We geared up and went with the Captain and reinforcements toward the sound of the guns. On the way, we learned we had one medivac from the combat. By the time we arrived, the gunfire had all but stopped. A KMC private had a gunshot wound, and we called in a medivac. After the medivac, we joined Sergeant Lee as the Koreans searched out the area.

We found a well camouflaged tunnel. The hole was only large enough to crawl into flat on your stomach. Sergeant Lee and I were standing by the tunnel mouth. He gave a command, and one of the Koreans threw a hand grenade into the opening. We took cover as the muffled detonation blew dirt out of the hole. Sergeant Lee started to leave when I asked him if they were going to search it. Sergeant Lee shook his head "no." I asked him why not. He said, making a cutting throat motion, "Maybe VC." Without thinking, I told him, "USMC would search." I hurt his pride, and rapidly blinking his eyes, he took off his flak jacket and helmet so he could fit inside the tunnel. He entered the tunnel head first with a flash light and a .45 held in front of him. Only after he was in did I realize that I might never see

Sergeant Lee again. I felt sick. After what seemed like a long time, he came out. I apologized profusely to Sergeant Lee and told him I had behaved very badly. As he brushed the dirt and spider webs off, he mumbled something about KMC and USMC and walked away. He could have ordered one of his men into the tunnel, but chose to risk himself instead. I would apologize again later and he forgave me. It's ironic: I couldn't speak when I keyed the handset for my first medivac, but yet I could speak when I should have kept my mouth shut. I had to correct that. Had anything happened to Sergeant Lee in that tunnel, I never would have forgiven myself. *That would be a nightmare I do not need.*

The next day, we had resupply, and John and I got mail. In addition to getting a letter from my family, I got a letter from either Debbie or her Mom every time we got mail. Today I got one from each. Debbie was a senior in the small school I had attended. *There were only twelve kids in my graduation class.* She was a cheerleader, and for some reason, many of the girls of that class wanted to be the most popular girl in school. They would do stupid and mean things to hurt and discredit each other. Sometimes Debbie was the swatter and sometimes she was the fly. She was the fly right now, and her and her Mother's letters went into great detail about how hard life was for Debbie. After what I had seen out here in the past couple of days, I had a hard time mustering up any sympathy. I was also writing to her swatters. Ok, I admit, I looked forward to getting mail from both of them. Enough said.

The rest of the operation passed with more of the same. There were a few medivacs from either sniper fire or booby traps, but it was otherwise uneventful. By the end of the operation, I had learned how to control myself on and off the radio.

I was raised on a cattle ranch and farm. I had pulled calves from cows having a difficult time giving birth. I had helped the vet and my Dad perform a c-section on a cow. I had the castration duties during branding. I had cleaned my share of barns and chicken houses. I had learned at an early age how to repress my revulsion of the task by concentrating on the task. I had seen and smelled blood and gore before. Over the course of my childhood, I had seen many things hurt and many things die. I hunted rabbits and coyotes from the time I was about fourteen or so, and I understood what a bullet could do to living flesh. Turns out, people and animals die very much in the same way. I am sure that because of my background, I could deal with the shock of badly wounded people a little better. I had learned how to push the horrors of war to a dark place in the back of my mind and concentrate on the job at hand. Sometimes it was more difficult than other times. For the first time in forty years, I have peeked into that dark place to see what I hid there long ago.

Although I still enjoy shooting, I quit hunting many years ago.

On the fifth day, we started back, retracing the route we came in on. We came to that open area where we had suffered all the booby trap victims the first day. I swallowed hard. This was the field where Moon and I almost bought the farm. I think we were more careful on the way out, and we made it without anyone getting hurt. The trucks were waiting for us by the time we got to the road, and we went home.

Sergeant Lee came over that evening and informed us that we were going on a fifteen day operation in a couple of days. That night, while I was writing letters, John and Sergeant Lee sat at the table across from me and composed a letter to Carolyn. John asked if he would like her to send him anything. Sergeant Lee insisted that was not necessary. After he thought about it for a little bit, he decided that he would like some "long sizes." Neither John nor I had heard that term before, and John asked him what a "long size" was. Sergeant Lee picked up a cigarette with his left hand, "Tombay (Korean word for cigarette)." He then extended his right index finger two inches beyond the tip of the cigarette, "long size." We figured out that he would like Carolyn to send some cigars. Sergeant Lee blinked a lot that night.

John

Relaxing at 26 Co. hooch

My first counter-part, John Staunton

With John and Sgt. Lee. Large Bunker in background is the Captain's bunker

26th Company

Chapter 6
The Holidays

Gettle and Don came out the next morning and brought our mail and a box of goodies. Gettle had scrounged up some "A" rations somewhere. We unpacked our stuff on our table. Our gift from Gettle was steaks, potatoes, onions, grapes, pop and a pint of chocolate milk each. It was a great and unexpected treat. Gettle told us he did this because he felt bad that we were going back out tomorrow. We thanked Gettle, and he and Don were on their way. John and I saved some of our food and took it over to Sergeant Lee. He thanked us, but he didn't seem that excited about American food. After Korean fare, it probably tasted pretty bland.

While we were sitting outside of Sergeant Lee's hooch, I noticed the biggest Korean Marine I had ever seen. He was a massive man that stood about six foot five. I asked Sergeant Lee about the big KMC. He replied that he was a new guy. Then after thinking about it a moment, he laughed, "Because he is bigger than most KMC, he is "Long Size." We all know how a nickname can stick. From then on I called him "Long Size." *Most American men would like the nickname "Long Size"; the large Korean Private did not like his nickname, and made a nasty face every time we addressed him as "Long Size."*

After having leftovers from our goodie box for dinner, we laid out all the gear we were carrying on the operation the next day. After making sure we were ready to go, we sat at the table and visited. I told John that I was thinking pretty seriously about extending in Vietnam for six months. I

The Holidays

explained all the good reasons, thirty days free leave anywhere in the free world, and even better, no inspections over here! John had only signed up for two years, and he would not have that many inspections left after he went home. More importantly, he explained, he had a wife and was expecting a baby soon. He felt that he had an obligation to stay as safe as possible, and he was thinking about asking for a transfer to Brigade. We both agreed that this probably was not the safest spot he could be in. He said that he had not mentioned this to anyone else, and he had mixed feelings. He loved 26th Company and would miss Sergeant Lee and me. John decided that he wasn't deciding right now.

The procedure was the same as my first operation. We boarded trucks which took us to 27th Company C.P. this time. There, we disembarked, deployed and swept to the northeast. We swept all day without an incident.

The closest thing we had to casualties was a Korean Radio operator and an Anglicoman. I was following a Korean radio operator through a knee-deep flooded rice paddy. One second I was watching his back, and the next second there was a foot of his ten foot whip antenna making little circular waves in the dirty water. He had stumbled into a large flooded bomb crater and would have drowned if one of his buddies had not been quick with a branch to help him out. I could not help but laugh at the shocked and dripping wet guy. I patted him on the back and told him he was a "submarine." He didn't think it was that funny.

It was late afternoon when we stopped to dig in for the night. John and I started to dig our bunker near where the Captain's was being built. Sergeant Lee was building his next door to us. There was a song going around in Vietnam then and one of the lines was: "The time came as it comes to all when you have to answer nature's call." That time had come, and I told John that I would be right back. Because I was a modest country farm kid, I decided to go over a small sandy hill to the northeast. I walked over the hill to where I thought no one could see me, dug a small hole and started my business.

Apparently, someone could see me. One of the very first things I learned in Vietnam was how to differentiate between the sound of an M-16 and that of an AK-47. From a wood line two or three hundred yards to the northeast, there was a long burst from an AK-47. At the same time I heard the gunfire, those rounds were impacting the ground nearby and buzzing overhead. I ran, as well as a guy can run with his pants down, over and down the hill and fell behind a sandbag wall with Sergeant Lee and John. Only then did the firing cease. *I have given this incident a lot of thought. I think the only reason they missed is that they were laughing too hard. Humor is my friend.*

As I rolled over on my back to pull my pants up, I caught the eyes of the Korean "submarine" radio operator crouched behind his bunker. He was pointing at me and laughing, the old "He who laughs last." I smiled back. Indeed, much of the company had seen me running with my pants down, and most were laughing including John and Sergeant Lee. Getting shot at and missed made me a little giddy, like I had gotten away with something.

For just a moment, the bad guys and the good guys were as one, both getting a laugh at my expense. Within thirty seconds or so after the firing had stopped, the Koreans were dropping mortar rounds into the woods where the shots had come from.

We took sporadic fire all night from that tree line. The next morning Lieutenant Kim informed me that they had requested an air strike on the offending woods at about 0800. I called Battalion and they confirmed it.

John and I crawled to the crown of the hill that I had run back down last night, and we waited for the spotter plane. We heard a small single engine plane come in from the north. "Kimchi two-three" made radio contact with us. He advised us that we had a flight of two F-4s coming on station and asked us for a situation briefing. We had checked and rechecked with Lieutenant Kim, so we felt confident that we understood how the Company was deployed. We advised the spotter plane of the "friendly positions." We then described the target. We gave him a compass bearing and distance to the target from our position. He asked for a smoke, and we threw out a yellow one. He acknowledged our yellow smoke. It was quiet for a moment while the spotter plane relayed that information to the jets. Only the hum of the small plane disturbed the silence. As he circled around, he made an approach to the target parallel to the Company's front line and fired two Willy Pete (white phosphorus) rockets into the woods about 300 yards away. White smoke bellowed up from the woods. He asked us if the Willy Pete was on target. We confirmed it as the target.

Then, from the southeast, two F-4s at low altitude roared directly over our yellow smoke and made a climbing left turn. I watched as they made a wide circle to line up on the same approach the spotter plane had taken. They came in low and together and both dropped double canisters of napalm. It was the first time I had seen napalm up close. It is one thing that Hollywood has a hard time overdoing. It was a ball of rolling flame and black smoke that dwarfed the trees. There were secondary explosions, a sign that something on the ground blew up.

The company was ready to move. I ran over and climbed on top of one of the LVTs, and we moved toward the smoldering woods. We didn't take any fire and entered the woods. The Koreans were searching out the area which looked like a camp.

The LVT had just rocked to a halt when a Korean shouted something and started firing to our left. I looked where he was aiming and saw a VC/NVA running away through the woods about fifty yards away. *VC were local guerrillas, VIET CONG, NVA were NORTH VIETNAMESE ARMY. It was often difficult to distinguish between the two.* I aimed and the LVT lurched forward. The shot went wild. The driver had also seen him and decided to give chase. We could see him ducking in and out of the cover as the LVT crashed through the brush and maneuvered around the trees. To our right, three or four Koreans on foot were also in the chase. The LVT's .30 machine gun, the three Koreans and I had all been firing at him, but so far he had dodged when he needed to dodge. He was running out of woods, where we would have an advantage, and, I guess he decided to make a stand. He turned toward the LVT and let off a burst. His rounds buzzed overhead as we were shooting at him. He missed. Some of us didn't.

I felt an odd primitive satisfaction that almost made me sick. *I don't know if I hit him, I don't want to know. A word here about the enemy we were fighting. I had developed the utmost respect for their courage, strength, commitment and their skill.*

I walked through one of the VC caches. The Koreans had found bags and bags of rice. There were also papers scattered about, including one I picked up that was an invitation for American service men to desert. They also captured a number of weapons, including SKS rifles, AK-47s, U.S made .30 carbines, B-40 rocket launchers, (something LVT guys dreaded) and piles of ammunition. We also captured two flags. One was red and blue with a yellow star, and the other was red with a yellow hammer and sickle. The Koreans gave John the first flag and me the latter as a souvenirs.

After fourteen days of snoopin' and poopin,' we came in on the 20th of November 1968. It was good to get home to our hooch. We got our mail, and on Thanksgiving we had a canned turkey that John's wife had sent. Sergeant Lee came over that night and told us that because of the company's performance on the last operation, we were being rewarded with RnR in DaNang. Sergeant Lee's excitement was contagious, and we got ready for the ride to China Beach in DaNang.

When a Korean Company goes on RnR, it looks very much like a Korean Company going on an operation, except there are more smiles on RnR. The Koreans were armed to the teeth with hand grenades hanging from flak jackets. All gave the right of way to that convoy that was on the way to China Beach. To a populace used to seeing military men and vehicles, the convoy still attracted attention as it passed. I proudly stood at the front of a box full of Korean Marines. The Korean Marines have a reputation of being a tough, badass bunch with their own rules of conduct. I felt like I was with an outlaw motorcycle gang.

We entered China Beach. There we learned that there were two China Beach Rest and Recuperation areas. There was a China Beach for the Americans, and separated by a tall barbed wire fence, there was a China Beach for the Koreans. Except for electricity, the quarters here were no better than where we had come from. But the beach was here, and the beer and kimchi flowed freely. The company was having a grand time running and playing in the surf. *The Koreans taught me that wealth is not necessary to be happy. Wealth is relative. I had seen piles and piles of boxes going home to Korea with the troops rotating home. Every individual KMC, based on rank, was allotted a large number of pounds (in the hundreds) that he could take home on the ship. Most of the boxes were K and C rations to feed their families in Korea.* John and I bunked with some of the Korean Lieutenants.

The second day, John and I decided to go over to the American side. We found a hole in the fence by the sea and walked into a different world. Whereas the Koreans only had the basics, the Americans seemed to have it all. We went to the club. A jute box was playing rock and roll, and USO girls were dancing with servicemen. John and I ordered a dozen cheeseburgers. What we couldn't eat, we were going to take back to our Korean friends. We sat at a table and watched the USO girls dancing with the servicemen. Guys were standing in line to dance with girls they would never look at back home. I know that the USO girls were there to improve moral. I just felt exploited. We finished a couple of burgers and fries and took the rest back to the Korean side with us.

We gave the fast food to Sergeant Lee and the Korean officers. They all seemed to make an attempt to enjoy it, but it became obvious that they didn't. They apologized. We told them it was ok, and that night we got drunk with the officers. In spite of the fly-ridden mess hall, the primitive sleeping quarters and facilities, and no hamburgers, John and I felt more at home with the Koreans and never went back to the American side. When it was time to go home, we all piled into the trucks and started home through the crowded streets of Da Nang.

I was in the front of the box of the second truck in the convoy. When we went anywhere in trucks, it was standing room only. I was watching the Koreans in the truck in front of me when they hit a large pothole. The KMCs rocked against each other, and a hand grenade was jarred loose. It fell out of the truck onto the pavement. We all watched in horror as our truck ran over the grenade. It shot out to the right, and hit a South Vietnamese soldier (ARVN) on a motor scooter. He freaked and wiped out, causing a chain reaction with more scooters, motorcycles and bicycles crashing. The grenade had bounced off the ARVN and was rolling back across the across the street. It emerged from under the third truck, creating the same chain reaction wipeouts on the oncoming traffic. People everywhere were diving for cover. We left pure chaos in our wake and drove on as if nothing had happened. It was like a scene out of an old "Charlie Chaplin" movie. The grenade didn't go off.

We had fun, but it was good to come home. I looked at my calendar, December 5th. One thing about operations, the time went quickly.

The next day, we moved to our new home base. This one was down the road west of LZ Dusty. The position was enclosed by bunkers, wire and claymores. Our hooch was almost exactly like our last one with the added feature of a hidden trap door that led into a small underground bunker. Nice selling point!

That night I received a letter from Sweet Ma. *I have called my Mother "Sweet Ma" since I was fifteen years old.* I learned that Johnny Wallen had sent her a letter asking for my address. That was great news. Johnny, the banjo player, and I had said goodbye in DaNang when we came in country. We had been exchanging letters, and he was in some nice safe job and hated it. A few weeks later, he told me he had volunteered for Force Recon and been accepted as one of their radio operators. I did not like reading that news at all. Force Recon was about as bad as it gets. He had sent a photo of him with his team, all painted up and ready to go. I had not heard from him since. I wrote to him that night. *I never heard from him again. Try as I might, I still have not been able to get in touch with him. When I visited "THE WALL" in Washington, D.C., I searched for his name. I was relieved when I couldn't find it. I continue to search.*

I also got letters from a number of girls, including Debbie and her mom. Almost every time I got mail, I got mail from them, and sometimes packages as well. Debbie informed me that she and a boy in her class were "going steady," but not to worry, it was not that kind of relationship. When is a "Dear John" not a "Dear John"? Sheesh... I continued to write to her, but I had little faith in our relationship.

We enjoyed our short stay in our hooch, and on the 8th

The Holidays

of December, at seven in the morning, we left on a five day operation. From our new C.P., we walked in extreme heat for what seemed like forever. The radio felt like it weighed a ton. I had no problem getting down whenever we took fire; it was just a little harder getting back up. Every time we took a break, I would take a couple of salt tablets, and I was drenched in sweat. We walked all day covering a variety of different terrains. We had three medivacs, one from a small booby trap and two heat stroke victims.

That evening, when we stopped and started to dig, in we had a firefight with Charlie (VC or spelled phonetically VICTOR CHARLIE) which lasted about four or five minutes. There were no friendly casualities, but it kept everyone on edge for a while.

The first thing I thought of, after the shooting stopped, was that night on leave when Dad told me about his company taking sniper fire one night while they were digging in. "Ok, Dad," I thought, "now I know what that feels like." I decided that I would just as soon take his word on what it was like to be shot.

I was always grateful for John. Sometimes, when it really got rough, one of us would say something stupid to make the other guy laugh. Ya gotta keep your sense of humor.

I had been with 26th Company long enough to feel like it was my home. I had wonderful friendships within the Company. The KMC were tough and brave. I could not ask for greater comrades-in-arms. Part of the deal if you extended was that you got to come back to the same unit. That was very important to me. This was the most stable I had felt since I joined the Marine Corps. Just as important, I felt that I was doing some good here.

John and I built our bunker. This time, we hoped that we got it right. We watched Sergeant Lee's bunker being built and tried to copy the design. Sergeant Lee would always come around and give our bunker a grade, "Bunker, maybe number four, maybe number five."

The next few days, we left in the morning and swept all day, returning to our "field bunker" in the late afternoon. I took my helmet liner out of my helmet and filled the helmet with water and soaked my feet. The Koreans were able to dig a shallow well for our water supply. When we made our last radio check with Battalion, Pete told us that we would not get mail until we went back to our C.P. in a couple more days.

On the seventh night of the five day operation, it rained. I was awakened when two of the bunker sandbags fell on me. I looked at my watch; it was 11:35 (2335), a long time till sunrise. I could see by flares going off that the poncho was again full of water. This time I crawled out of the bunker and using my helmet, bailed the water out. The bunker lasted through the night, and the next day when we got back from our daily sweep, we repaired our bunker. This time we asked Sergeant Lee what we were doing wrong. His bunkers never failed.

The night of the 20th, one of our ambush teams tagged a VC group and killed seven bad guys and captured a number of weapons and grenades. On the 21st of December, Lieutenant Kim told us we were going to be out here for another week, at least through Christmas.

The Holidays

The HQ group, where we stayed, did not go out every day. We had received resupply and mail. I asked Battalion to send out my new $80 Zenith Transistor Radio. Armies have always loved their music, and we were no exception. When we were not doing anything during the day, we sat by our bunker listening to music from our one radio station. The Disk Jockeys would try and satisfy as many people as possible, and there was a wide variety of musical genres. Music seemed to be very important to all of us. The Koreans also had a radio station located at Brigade. I am sure it was not very powerful, but wherever I went, it did a good job of getting their music out. Our music was always competing with their music. Today, we listened to Christmas music all day.

On the 23rd there was a cease-fire until 1800 on the 25th. I was planning to have a Christmas Eve dinner of rice, kimchi and soup. When I checked in with Battalion, they informed me that at 1700 we had two CH-46s coming in with emergency resupply. I knew nothing about the Koreans needing resupply, but I told them I would be standing by. The helicopters made radio contact *(don't forget to squeeze and jiggle your throat)*,

"Scorcher Bravo, this is Santa Clause two nine."

We landed the helicopter, and two crewmen ran off with large boxes of food, Christmas dinner. I wrote a letter to my parents and told them all that we had received: mashed potatoes and gravy, sweet potatoes, dressing, turkey, beef, green beans, shrimp and sauce, rolls and butter, eggnog, cherry turnovers, oranges, apples and a bag of Christmas candy and cookies for both of us.

The Koreans were shocked. John and I were still just PFCs. It seemed unreal that a country could be so rich that it was willing to spend that much in resources for two PFCs. I couldn't agree more, and I was very proud and grateful. It was a great Christmas. Again, there was more food than John and I could possibly eat, but we tried. We offered to share with our KMC friends, but they were not interested. I guess the cold greasy hamburgers we had given them on RnR bummed them out on American food.

At 1800 (6PM) on the 25th, the cease fire ended, and it seemed like every cannon in the country fired. The war was back on. We were still on the operation on NEW YEARS DAY, 1969 and received another dinner much like the Christmas Dinner. What a country!

On the 3rd of January, the operation ended, and we finally went back to our rear CP to a very dusty bunker. John had decided that he was tired of being shot at and looking for booby traps, and that he was going to ask for a transfer into Brigade. I hated to see him go, but I understood that he had a wife who was expecting a baby. He had been with 26th Company since we had arrived with the Koreans. Peter Plummer became my new counterpart.

The Holidays

Moon, with something they killed for dinner and me in rice paddy

With Lt. Kim and Battalion G-3 Captain

With Lt. Kim, Battalion G-3 Captain and John

The Holidays

The paper I picked up in one of the caches.

Inside

— PRESS FOR YOUR EVACUATION FROM South VIETNAM TO REJOIN YOUR FAMILIES AND ENJOY THE SWEETNESS OF A PEACEFUL HAPPY LIFE !

— Try to avoid your families such grief and suffering as that has fallen to tens of thousands of American mothers who lost their sons and wives who lost their husbands in the U.S. aggressive war in South Vietnam.

— NO FIGHTING AND DYING FOR JOHNSON CLIQUE'S PROFIT !

— When being sent to the battlefront, lay down your arms and pass over to the Liberation Army's side.

You'll be treated with kindness and humanity and will be helped to return home if you wish to.

Living With Dragons

John and KMC

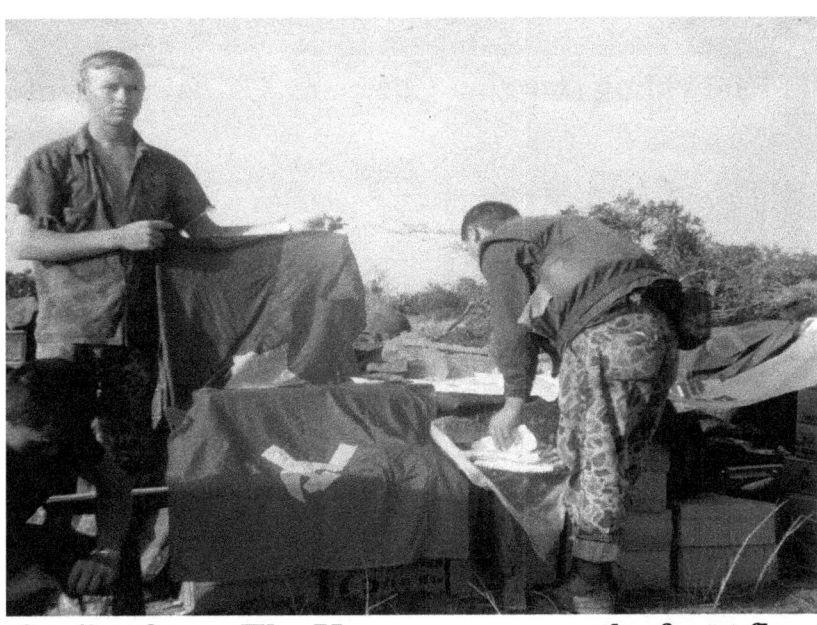

Spoils of war. The Koreans gave me the front flag

The Holidays

**Going on RnR
Lt. Kim riding shotgun, Company Captain in center**

Dinner time, December 1968

Chapter 7
The Lost Helmet

Peter had purchased a portable TV when he went to DaNang the last time, and he brought it out with him. Our one TV Station, Armed Forces Network, started broadcasting at 1:00 PM. The shows included: BIG VALLEY, COMBAT, GUNSMOKE, BONANZA, STAR TREK, DRAGNET and MISSION IMPOSSIBLE. We did not have electricity, but we had figured out how to power it off Prick 25 radio batteries. It helped pass the time. We also spent a lot of time listening to AFVN (Armed Forces Viet Nam) radio. In addition to the music, they devoted a lot of airtime to "public service" messages, such as "how to watch out for booby traps" and "the dangers of visiting houses of ill-repute." One of the more entertaining messages concerned malaria:

Announcer: "A clerk is busy in his tent typing when he hears a noise. He turns and sees a Vampire standing behind him," (in a Boris Karlof voice):

"Goud even-ning."

"Who are you?" asks the clerk.

"Have you taken your malaria pill today?"

"No, of course not, they taste bad."

"Gooud!" (and then, with a sinister laugh and the victim's scream, the vampire bites the clerk). Announcer: "And we have another victim of malaria; take your malaria pill!"

Those pills did taste bad. But the mogies (Korean word for mosquitoes) were as thick at night as the flies were in the day. Every night, we slept with our mogie nets over us, and we always used the nasty, oily, smelly mogie juice (mosquito repellent).

I got an American flag from my grandparents. On the 5th of January, we went out on another operation, and the LVT guys flew that flag on their radio antenna. We left the C.P. in the rain, and it rained off and on for the next four days. It was an active operation, and we had a number of medivacs. We were attacked the third night out by machine guns, small arms and B-40 rockets. Lt. Kim relayed that the captain would like a spooky gunship. We requested and received a Spooky. Spooky, or Puff the Magic Dragon gunships, were converted cargo planes armed with mini-guns that had an awesome rate of fire of 6,000 rounds per minute. In addition to his guns, he also carried flares. The Air Force also had converted some of the same type of planes into flare ships, which were not armed. Until he fired, the enemy would not know if it was a flare ship or a gunship. We could talk directly to the plane and give him all the necessary information which included location of friendlies and the target area. That information had to be very precise. I had heard of a company in a different battalion that had a Korean platoon badly shot up by a short burst from Spooky. Spooky was an impressive weapon. When he opened fire, it was not with a "bang-bang" but a "BUZZZZZ." His tracers looked like a "Star Trek" laser burning the earth through the night sky. The firefight ended shortly after he opened fire. After about an hour, Spooky was relieved by a flare ship.

Pete and I took turns sleeping and directing the flare ship until about four in the morning. The large lumbering airplane flew in a large circle and dropped a flare on each pass. The flares kept it pretty well lit up, and we had to tell him where we wanted the next flare dropped. We received no more incoming that night. The next morning, we swept the area and found twenty-one dead VC/NVA and many weapons. We had medivacs and/or resupply on almost a daily basis.

We came in from the operation on the 13th of Jan. The LVT I was riding on made a turn to go to their base, while the other one continued to our Rear C.P. I was on the wrong LVT, so as it passed, I jumped from one to the other. They slowed down for my jump, but I lost my helmet as I made the leap. No problem, helmets were easy to come by, and I didn't ask them to stop.

Sergeant Lee told us we were going back out on the 15th to provide security for another company's CP while they were on an operation. We had a check list of stuff we had to take on every operation. That list included: weapons, radio, extra batteries, map, compass and always the frequency book. The frequency book was a "classified" code book that contained codes for switching to different frequencies. Whenever we called in anything, PAST ONE FOUR would advise us which frequency we should use to talk to the helicopters etc. I always kept that book in my helmet. Remember my helmet. Oh no.

They changed the codes every so often and it was due to change. Captain Harring and Gettle came out from Battalion to give us the latest version of the book, and I told

The Lost Helmet

the Captain what happened to the last one. He informed me that it was a very bad thing to lose a classified document. I knew that, and I felt terrible. I was worried about what punishment I might face. There was no damage done as we had just changed books, but it was the principle of the thing. He didn't know what might happen to me, but said he would try to defend me. We got our new book and left for 10th Company CP.

10th Company provided security for the Artillery Battalion located in an old French fort on the outskirts of the town of Hoi An. Pete and I settled into the Anglicoman bunker. Because it was an artillery battalion, all the bunkers were constructed of empty artillery ammo boxes filled with sand. At first, Pete and I thought that a wooden bunker was nicer than a sandbag bunker. After a few nights, we realized that rats also liked it here. They were thick, and at night we could hear them scurrying through the ammo boxes that made up our walls. They almost drove Pete and me mad.

One night, I sat up in my cot and banged on the wall and screamed at them, "Rats, this is not your bunker, this is my bunker!" Pete had a .357 cowboy revolver and holster he had received from home. One night, the rats had an extra large party, and it was keeping us awake. We heard one going through our c-rat box, and Pete turned on his flashlight. I looked over and saw that he had his .357 out. I shouted "No Pete!" just as he fired. The retort of that large revolver in that tiny bunker left my ears ringing. He killed the rat and a can of c-rat peaches. Some Koreans came running over, and Pete told them what he had done. With my ears still ringing, I couldn't hear the rats anymore, and I went to sleep. It seemed the Koreans always had a number of artillery fire missions every night. Between the outgoing artillery fire and the rats, sleep was difficult at 10th Company C.P.

The weather was hot, and it was pretty boring here; so one day, Pete and Sergeant Lee decided that they were going to walk downtown into Hoi An and visit a skivvy house. I told them, like I told everyone visiting such a house, that they would catch something. Like everyone else, they didn't listen to me. They left early in the morning, and after a hot day, they returned late in the afternoon. They were both beat from the long hot walk. I asked Sergeant Lee if he enjoyed himself. He replied, "All day walk and walk and walk, oopsa (no, none, zero) boom boom."

I had gone to Sergeant Lee and the Korean officers and told them about the lost helmet and the code book inside of it. Sergeant Lee could see that I was concerned. Putting his hands together as if in handcuffs, he asked, "Maybe Anglicoman Scott go to monkey house (jail)?" I shrugged and told him, "Maybe." I had a faint hope that maybe a KMC had found it and turned it in. I explained the markings on the helmet, an arrow pointing up with "ONE WAY" printed underneath it. They sympathized with me and promised to look for it. Of all the things I worried about in Vietnam, losing that code book worried me the most. I thought of the consequences that might come of my carelessness, busted and/or transferred to some other USMC outfit, or even jail? I would rather have been shot than face any of those possibilities.

One night, Sergeant Lee woke us and told us we had a medivac. We always tried to get as much information on the way as we could from Sergeant Lee. We asked him "Booby trap?" He shook his head "no." "Snipie?" (sniper) Again, he

The Lost Helmet

shook his head "no." The medivac was within the compound, and we came upon a KMC private lying on the ground screaming. He only had a foot wound, and normally the Koreans gave their wounded enough morphine that they had no pain. Not only did this wounded Korean not get morphine, but he was being yelled at, kicked and hit with a stick by a Korean Lieutenant. He had shot himself in the foot, probably an accident, maybe not, but either way the Korean Lieutenant was unhappy. We told them that they would have to wait until morning as he was only a routine medivac. That was OK with the Lieutenant. He wanted this guy to hurt for a while longer.

Everyday, I asked Lieutenant Kim about the helmet. To help in the search, I gave him a sketch of the markings I had on my helmet. Everyday, Lieutenant Kim would sadly reply that they had not found it. I prayed that God would help me out of this jam I had put myself in.

A few days later, when I made the morning radio check with Battalion, they told me that Captain Harring and Gettle were coming out to see us. I felt sure that I would be placed under arrest and taken back with them. I found Sergeant Lee and told him that my Captain was coming out, and I may have to go back with them, so, this may be goodbye. Lieutenant Kim was there when they pulled up in Banard, the truck, and he told us that the Korean Captain would like us all to come to his bunker. We went into the well furnished bunker and had a seat with all the Korean officers. A couple of KMC privates brought us cold beers. Lieutenant Kim translated for the Korean Captain. He addressed Captain Harring:

"You know Anglicoman Scott lose important radio

paper?"

Captain Harring replied in a very cool tone that he did know about the paper. The Korean Captain said something to Lieutenant Kim who then translated, "My Captain said that he thinks Anglicoman Scott is good man." Lieutenant Kim surprised us all then when he said that they had found the helmet. He summoned one of the KMC privates to hand it over to Captain Harring. It looked very much like the one I had sketched. Captain Harring took the helmet and looked at the inside. He asked about the code book. Lieutenant Kim explained, "KMC private see paper in helmet. But he cannot read English, so he use paper to start fire to cook rice." I almost laughed. Captain Harring was silent for a moment, probably trying hard not to laugh too, "Would this man sign papers stating that he burned them?" Lieutenant Kim replied that he didn't think that would be problem. A few minutes later, they brought in a non-English speaking KMC private that looked scared to death. Lieutenant Kim gave him the paper Captain Harring had drawn up and had him sign it. Then to the KMC private's great relief, he was dismissed.

I am sure that Captain Harring didn't believe a word of it, but he smiled, and said "Ok, Anglicoman Scott not in trouble."

God does indeed move in mysterious ways.

Pete had extended for six more months in Vietnam. He was going on RnR to Australia on the 25th. I had volunteered to extend for six months in Vietnam as well and was waiting to see if it was approved. John sent out letters and cigars (long sizes) from his sister for Sergeant Lee. Pete

The Lost Helmet

and I helped him smoke those cigars and answer those letters.

10th Company came back, and we packed up and moved a little way into Hoi An to an ARVN compound by the river. We were to hold their compound while the South Vietnamese soldiers were gone somewhere. For the most part, the days were quiet, and we swam in the river and just hung out. The ground was littered with thousands of never-fired .30 carbine rounds. I found a good board and practiced batting those rounds into the river, trying to hit some of the sampan traffic. I batted hundreds of those rounds into the river. I suppose that it is possible that one could have gone off. Still, compared to the rest of the dangers I had every day, I felt it was not a risk. I never hit a sampan, but they would row a little faster when they saw the splashes nearby. *I probably tipped the scale a little to the wrong side. It may be that I was adopting the attitude of the people I was serving with. I really never came that close to hitting them.*

We spent a lot of time swimming in the dirty river. Sergeant Lee, Pete and I stripped down to our skivvies and tiptoed through a small opening in the wire and waded into the river.

The banks of the river were steep, and we were over our heads only feet from the shore. We started swimming and playing in the river. I had never been a good swimmer, and I was getting tired, so I decided to swim to shore and rest. Sergeant Lee decided that it would be fun to prevent me from swimming to shore and maintained a "blocking" position in front of me. I was becoming desperate while I continued to try to swim around Sergeant Lee. I could not, under any circumstances, let the many Koreans standing on the bank see me beg. Pete saw my dilemma and swam over to the side of Sergeant Lee. Using Pete as a shield, I swam around him and reached the bank of the river. I climbed out and sat on the bank as I got my breath back. I watched Pete and Sergeant Lee swimming.

Pete had now become the "blocking force" in front of Sergeant Lee. Sergeant Lee was a good swimmer, but Pete, who was from a coastal town in Maine, was a great swimmer. Soon Sergeant Lee was tiring and tried to exit the river. Pete blocked his every move. Sergeant Lee's struggle to reach dry land had reached a critical point. Gasping, he cried to Pete, "Peter, please, you want me swallow water?" Pete reminded Sergeant Lee how he wouldn't let me pass earlier. Sergeant Lee apologized. Pete let him pass, and the three of us sat on the bank and rested.

One afternoon, Pete, Sergeant Lee and I were standing and visiting in the shade of the only tree in the compound. We heard the nearby unmistakable crack of an AK-47 at the same moment that we heard the sickening thump of the round hitting something soft but solid. The instant we heard the round, we were on the ground, and we all expected that one of us was not getting up. We looked at each other and were surprised that the "thump" we heard had not been one of us. It had struck the tree we were standing around. We scampered behind the shelter of a nearby bunker. There is nothing quite as exciting as getting "shot at and missed," and we shared a nervous laugh.

I took a short walk along the barbed wire along the river. I saw something hanging in the wire. As I walked closer, I saw a black, shriveled hand from a previous attack hanging in the wire. I stared at the hand for a moment. It

The Lost Helmet

only stirred a mild curiosity.

A couple of nights later, we were awakened by a firefight in the distance. I got up and turned on my radio to see what was happening. 7th Company was engaged with "Charlie." After the firefight was over, the Anglicomen in that company had medivacs, and I watched and listened as the CH-46s came in. I heard the Anglicoman tell the helicopters that he was turning on his strobe light. Then, the door gunner of one of the choppers started firing. The Anglicoman was screaming that they were firing at the strobe light. Later, I met Joe Medina, the guy holding the strobe. While talking about the incident, Joe said he kept pushing the button to shut it off, and then it would blink again. "I threw that fu.ker as far as I could and ran the other way!" The door gunner stopped firing, and no one was hurt. The chopper pilot apologized and asked if anyone had been hit. The Anglicoman said that no one was hit, but that they owed him one strobe light. It was a near miss for Joe.

On the 22nd of March, Battalion relieved Pete and me. We went back to Battalion for a rest in a more secure area.

Gettle and I took the truck into Brigade to get the mail and all of my checks that I hadn't gotten while I was on operations for months. When we walked into the office, the Gunny Sergeant called someone on a land line, and said "Sir, Leis is here." After a pause, he said "Yes sir, we will be right over." Gettle and I followed the Gunny out the hooch to the Major's office. I had never personally talked to the man, and why would he want to see me? Then, like a cold slap, that "helmet thing" smacked me. "Now, I go to jail" I thought. We walked into the Major's office and snapped to attention. The Major then read my promotion papers and pinned my

Lance Corporal "stripe over crossed rifles" on my collars. I had been Lance Corporal since the first of February, but they had not had a chance to give it to me. I was thrilled to be a Lance Corporal.

Pete left the next day to go on his RnR in Australia. Don, Gettle and I played "RISK" that night until I went on radio watch.

It was during radio watch that I wrote many of my letters. I was corresponding with a number of girls. Two of the girls, Peggy and Diane, were from my high school and in the same class as Debbie. One of my old high school friends had given my name to a girl at his college. Her name was Irene, and she wrote nice letters and even sent a couple of packages.

We got a list of girls that wanted to write to a serviceman in Vietnam, so I picked one out and wrote to her. She answered my letter and was very excited. She said that she had never written to a Lieutenant Colonel before! I couldn't figure out what she was talking about. I guess that my return address rank "L/Cpl" looked like "Lt Col" to her. I wrote back and explained that I was not a Lieutenant Colonel but a Lance Corporal, and that was even cooler! She never wrote back.

I suppose that it was because of girls like that we decided we needed a little payback. We had received someone's hometown newspaper that was delivered to us by mistake. We read the misdelivered newspaper and found that there was a beauty contest going on in this little town. There were photos, small essays and addresses of all the contestants, and we decided to judge them. After a debate of the imagined good and bad qualities of the ten contestants, we voted upon the winner, runner up and the least likely to win. We felt like the "least likely" would get nothing, so we collected $10 and sent her a "LEAST LIKELY TO WIN AWARD." We probably created a war protester. *Sometimes, maybe because of our isolation with the Korean Marines and the war protests going on back home, we felt like it was "Us vs. The World."*

A few months earlier, the Anglicomen with 27th Company had captured a baby dog and pig. They brought them into Battalion since they could be cared for here better than out at the Company. We named the puppy Wally, and the pig was named Gunnery Sergeant Wilma Dog. Wally became a casualty when he was run over by a truck about a month later.

Gunny was doing well and she had grown up into a big pig. She ate c-rations and loved beer, although she got a little cranky when she had too much to drink. Gettle and I made her a Marine Corps cover (hat) with gunny stripes pinned on it. She didn't like the cover at first, but she got used to it. One day we noticed she was limping. She probably got kicked by a Korean. Gettle and I loaded her into Banard, and we went to Brigade to see our Navy Corpsman. I got my shots caught up, and he put Gunny's leg in a splint. She had a full recovery. She was known throughout the Brigade, and the Anglico Major came out to see her.

I was standing watch on April Fool's Day. I decided that I owed Don one for giving me my nickname, Worm. I called down to the hooch on the field telephone at 0001 on April 1st. I had them wake up Don, and I told him that he had to come down to the TOC because he had an important call from Brigade. He wanted to know what the problem was, and I told him I had no idea, but he had better hurry down here. A few minutes later, he walked into the TOC, and I handed him a folded piece of paper. He opened it up to read, "April Fools Day Donny." He read the note and looked up at me, shook his head and walked out. The Captain called a few minutes later and told me that he thought that was a good April Fools joke.

Don still had not sold his .38, and the bidding was up to $100. I guess he was holding out for the highest bid until he rotated back to the U.S. Everyday, Don, Gettle and I played a game of RISK. I had achieved the title of FIELD MARSHAL ERWIN WORMAL and was a feared and respected RISK opponent.

The 26th Company Captain requested me, and on the 10th of May, I went back out to 26th Company.

(Left to Right) Jeff Graves, Lt. Kim, Capt. Lee and Joe Medina
7th Company (Joe Photo)

With Pete at the Artillery Battalion

Randy holding babies Wally and Guns at 27th Co.

Scottie and Korean USO girl

Sergeant Lee and Pete

The Lost Helmet

With Guns and Banard, the truck

KMC Platoon Lieutenant

The Lost Helmet

Chapter 8
Back in the Field

I joined Scottie (Moses C. Scott) at 26th Co. on the 10th of May. Scottie was a black Marine from Detroit. I was raised in northeast Colorado on a farm and ranch and had never even talked to a black man before boot camp. It was great to be with Scottie. We had many discussions about the race riots going on back home, and both of us hated racism. He had a great sense of humor, and we had become close friends. We left the next day for what was supposed to be a five day operation. Our Company, 26th Company, was ordered to reinforce 25th Company, and together operate in an area to the north of Brigade C.P. called "the horseshoe" (a bend in a river that resembled a horseshoe). We were cooperating with USMC units to the north. DaNang was taking rockets from that area on an almost nightly basis, and we were sent out to disrupt that political no-no. Indeed, when I was back at Brigade, we could see rockets being launched from that area toward DaNang.

We were following the same path that 25th Company had taken two days earlier. We walked past a burned out LVT on the trail. The LVT had been with 25th Company when it was hit by a B-40 RPG (Rocket Propelled Grenade), and some of the crew had been killed and wounded. As always, we had two LVTs with us. They steered around the blackened LVT that some of their friends had died in.

Twenty-five yards up the trail, I saw a wild pig run away as the amtracks approached. I saw that the pig had been eating a two-day dead NVA soldier; probably the guy that had fired the rocket. Then, both LVTs ran over the remains of the body. I almost gagged at the sight and smell. I held my breath and faced forward. The Koreans shot the pig for soup.

That night, after we built our bunker, Scottie and I went over to the LVTs and offered our condolences to the crews. Then we joined them for cards inside their armored vehicle. It is easier to have a good game of cards with more than two people. As I mentioned earlier, we had a great relationship with the amtrac guys.

In the days that followed, we ran a lot of medivacs, resupply missions and called in air support in the form of Huey gunships and jets. In addition to killing a bunch of bad guys, we captured many weapons, rice caches, and a few prisoners. We also found some rockets which the Koreans blew in place. Lieutenant Kim gave me one of the captured SKS Chinese rifles with a bayonet and a NVA belt buckle. The rocket fire on DaNang ceased. We probably suffered more casualties stopping the rocket fire than had they hit DaNang. But when DaNang was hit by rockets, Walter Cronkite talked about it that night. When twenty Koreans died, no one heard about it; politics.

On the 17th of May, when I made my morning "radio check" with Battalion, Don informed me that my extension had been approved, and my new rotation date to go back to the U.S. was May 6th, 1970. My special leave, which amounted to 30 days free leave anywhere in the free world, was scheduled for the 1st of August. I started the countdown to my special leave at "85 Days!"

On the 20th of May, 25th Company ended their part of the operation and went back out the same way we had come into this area. The next day we followed. I rode on an LVT as we followed the same path out as we had come in on. Up ahead, I saw the destroyed LVT I had walked past the first day. Out of a morbid curiosity, I looked for the dead NVA soldier. I almost missed him. 25th Company's amtracks had run over him again on the way out, and by now, he was almost a part of the ground. After we drove over him, he was truly "dust to dust."

We rode the LVTs back to our rear C.P. Scottie and I carried our gear into our hooch, the one with the hidden bunker. Scottie was due to go on RnR, so Gettle drove out with my mail and Scottie's replacement. My new counterpart was a guy named Holt. I knew Holt the least of all the Anglicomen with 5th Battalion. I had heard that he had a reputation of being somewhat of a blowhard and hot tempered. Although we never became close, we got along well enough. The two LVTs that operated with us on the last operation went back to their base for a day to service their machines. They came back out to our C.P. the next day, since we were to leave again soon on another operation.

Holt and I were sitting at the table playing poker when we decided to take a grenade apart. The spoon assembly unscrewed from the base. There was a small tube blasting cap attached to the assembly. We pulled the pin and threw the spoon assembly into our underground bunker. There was a small pop! We then put the spoon back into the assembly and screwed it back on the body of the grenade. We pulled the pin and threw the grenade into our bunker cellar. Nothing, we had an inert grenade. Ok, what do we do with an inert grenade?

The LVT guys came over that night to play cards with

us. They came with beer, and the six of us sat down at our table and played cards. The dummy grenade was on the table. *We had marked the dummy and had stored away all of the live grenades to make sure the joke was not on us.* After we had been playing cards for a while and had a few beers, Holt started one of his stupid gross stories about his RnR in Hong Kong. It was easy for me to play my part.

"Holt," I almost spit out, "you're full of sh.t." That started a well rehearsed exchange between the two of us. After a little more name calling, he picked up the dummy grenade. The LVT guys were getting a little nervous by now and tried to calm Holt down. He pulled the pin that held the spoon. Our guests scooted their chairs back from the table. I laughed and told him "No balls." The spoon made a "sprong" noise as he let it fly. In an instant, the four amtrack guys were falling over the chairs and each other trying to get out the door. When it became obvious that the building was not blowing up, they came back in, kinda angry and kinda laughing. It was a rotten thing to do. And probably stupid. I have never claimed that I never did anything foolish.

Mom had written to me and wanted to know why in the world I had extended my time over here. I answered, "Partly patriotism, partly money, partly adventure and partly foolish."

On the 23rd of May, we left our C.P. for another operation. We were trucked out to 27th Company and at 0700 started sweeping to the west. We had been walking for about two hours when there was a massive explosion to our left front about 150 yards into the woods. Sergeant Lee, Holt and I ran toward the black cloud.

A KMC platoon had triggered a previously unexploded American 500 pound bomb that had been converted into a booby trap. It worked better as a booby trap than it did as a bomb. There were many dead, many close to death and many with less serious wounds. The platoon Lieutenant was slightly wounded, but had refused aid and was assisting in the care of his men. It was a grim scene. The largest part we found to medivac of the guy who had triggered the bomb was one of his boots in a tree. Holt started to call in the medivac, and I looked for a LZ.

I found a small open space in the trees close by that I felt was the best choice for a LZ. I started to search it out when I noticed a KMC with a mine detector. I called him over and explained that I would like him to help me search out the zone. I walked by his side and pointed to areas I wanted him to search. He was pretty relaxed about the process and was chatting with me while he was swinging the mine detector over the ground. All of a sudden, he stopped as he heard a buzzing noise in his earphones. His eyes were big as he pointed to the ground. Sure enough, we had found another big one. We cleared the area, and the Koreans blew up the booby trap. We continued to search my zone until I was satisfied that it was safe. While we waited for the helicopters, another wounded Korean died.

Two CH-46s approached from the North. I stood in the zone while Holt gave them the zone brief. Holt yelled for me to pop a smoke grenade. I threw out a red one. One of the CH-46s flew cover and the other started in. He came in too high and circled low to my right to make another approach. His propeller wash set off a small booby trap in the trees as he circled around. We ducked. No one was hurt by the booby trap, but the chase helicopter saw the explosion and wanted to know what it was. Holt told them that it was a booby trap. "Booby trap!" the pilot yelled, "You were supposed to search that zone!" Holt explained that the booby trap was not in the zone, and that the helicopter had set it off in the trees.

I guided the helicopter in, and the Koreans loaded all of the dead and wounded on board. The wounded Lieutenant refused to be medivaced until his Captain insisted. The CH-46 lifted off, and the noise and dust slowly subsided.

I walked over to Holt and noticed that he was rubbing his left eye. I asked what was wrong, and he said that his eye hurt. I looked in his eye, and I saw nothing out of the ordinary. He continued to insist that something was in his eye, maybe even shrapnel from the booby trap the helicopter had set off. I looked at his eye again, and I told him it was probably just dust. He felt sure that he needed medical attention and within fifteen minutes, he left with one of the LVTs going back to the C.P. for fuel and supplies.

Shortly after he left, the Koreans triggered another booby trap a couple hundred yards away, and I had another medivac. I stood in my new LZ with my radio and called it in. It was now about noon. The Company HQ group had not moved since the first booby trap, and I came back after the second medivac. I was hot, tired and dirty from all the dust. I dropped all of my gear, sat down on the LVT ramp, lit a cigarette and closed my eyes.

I was startled by someone playing with my chest hair. I opened my eyes to see Long Size playing with the hair on my chest and talking to his friends. *Koreans normally do not have chest hair and some found it fascinating.* I was enraged and snarled at him as I put my cigarette out on his bare chest.

He jumped back screaming and brushing his chest. I laughed for the first time that day. My laughing only angered him more, and he grabbed a stick and started toward me. Just as angry, I grabbed a bigger stick and moved to meet his attack. Had Sergeant Lee not jumped between us just then, Long Size probably would have killed me. He gave Long Size and me a good chewing out. *I have thought about Sergeant Lee's reaction. I probably saved Long Size from getting Kodabaca. He couldn't punish just one of us. Had I been Korean, we would both have had Kodabaca.* Long Size and I glared at each other. Whenever we saw each other after that, we would make obscene gestures, call each other nasty Korean names and hiss.

That afternoon, I was taking a nap in the shade of one the LVTs when someone kicked my foot. Ready to fight, I jumped up. It was Don; he had hitched a ride out with the LVT that had gone back for supplies. I was never happier to see anyone in my life. He was a short-timer with a little more than a month left before he went home, but had volunteered to come out and be with me. I was moved and grateful. The Company went back in after a couple more days, and Don and I both went into Battalion for a rest.

A few days later, 26th Company requested that I come back out to go on RnR with them to China Beach again. Holt had recovered from his wound, and we went to China Beach with 26th Company. This RnR was much like the first one. Holt and I only went over to the American side once for hamburgers and spent the rest of the time with the Koreans. On June 1st, we came back from RnR, and I went back to Battalion.

I resumed my Battalion duties which consisted only

of radio watch. One of the guys was going to DaNang and, at the moment, he had no money. He asked to borrow $5. I hesitated, "No, I know what you will do with it, and you'll catch something." He insisted that I give him $5, and that he was not going to catch anything. I gave him the $5. He came back from DaNang, and a couple of days later, he had a rash on his manhood. I told him, "I told you so." He called me weak because I had given him the $5.

We were told that if a Marine had to be treated for a social disease by a U.S. Navy Corpsman that it went on that Marine's record. He didn't want anything like that on his record, so he decided to go to the Korean Corpsman. The Korean Corpsman gave him a shot of penicillin every day for a week, yet the rash didn't go away, and he was becoming concerned. I tried to convince him that he had better go in and see the American Corpsman. He decided that I was right, and he went in to see Doc at Brigade. When he came back, he was madder than hops. After a week of shots from the Koreans, the "rash on his manhood" had been diagnosed as heat rash. The vast majority of us thought it was really funny.

Pete came back from RnR in Australia. He had a good time and told me all the details. He had spent about $500. I decided that I was not going on my RnR. I wanted to save my money to buy a car when I got home, and I was afraid I might do something that I didn't want to do on RnR. RnR (Rest and Recuperation) was also referred to as InI (Intoxication and Intercourse), and I didn't want to catch anything.

I had heard that two of the Anglicomen assigned to a company in a different Battalion went on RnR together to

Australia. They both ended up going there for their special leave and their second RnR. They got an early out of the Marine Corps when they left Vietnam and moved to Australia and started a sheep ranch. I never met the guys, and I got this information at best, second hand. I believe it to be true, but maybe, I just want it to be true.

One morning, some Koreans were down on the beach target practicing by shooting at empty k-ration cans. Pete and I decided to join them and show them some good USMC marksmanship. Pete strapped on his .357 in his cowboy holster, and we walked down to where the Koreans were shooting their M-16s. They noticed us walking up and were excided to see Pete and his cowboy gun. Pete paused, and with a draw that would have challenged Clint Eastwood, shot from the hip and hit one of the cans about fifty feet away. The Koreans cheered and clapped. Pete and I stood in shock at the shot. Pete recovered from his surprise, twirled his revolver on his finger and holstered it. We had to turn and walk away. Any further shooting on our part would only have hurt our image. I am sure that the word got out that Anglicoman Peter was just like John Wayne.

Don and Gettle were due to rotate back to the U.S., and I gave Don my NVA belt buckle. Gettle wanted to buy a new amplifier before he went home, but he had sent his money home, so I lent him $300. He was going to mail my folks the $300 when he got back to the States. I also gave him my SKS bayonet as a going away present. We played our last game of RISK together.

On the 10th of June, Pete and I went out to 26th Company for what was to be a long operation. This time we had two USMC bulldozers in addition to the two LVTs. As always, we had medivacs and had to run air strikes. We reached the river and set up camp. We were the "anvil" and were going to stay in this position for the duration of the operation. The USMC bulldozers proceeded to tear up the landscape to destroy VC bunkers, tunnel systems and deny the enemy cover and concealment.

Pete and I found a nice grassy area by the river to call in our daily resupply. We were happy with the LZ because the grass would keep the dust down when the helicopters came in. The LVTs parked about 25 yards away from the river. Pete and I built our bunker about 100 yards away near the Captain's bunker. The operation was a lax one with very little for us to do, and we spent a lot of time down by the river with the LVT guys.

Sergeant Lee had been awarded a medal for capturing a NVA armed with an M-14 rifle breathing through a reed under water. I gave him my congratulations. Sergeant Lee had been in country for fifteen months and was getting short with only about thirty-six days before he went home. He told us that he didn't want to go out to the medivacs with us anymore. I told him I would miss his help, but I understood. I didn't want to go out to the medivacs anymore either.

Long Size and I had grown bored of making obscene gestures and cussing and hissing at each other on sight. Still, he spoke no English, and we had nothing to do with each other.

We got our mail almost on a daily basis when we called in our resupply helicopters. I received another "Dear John" letter from Debbie. I had already written that relationship off, and I was not affected in the least.

It was a long and elaborate letter that explained how she had found her true love, and that we were just not meant to be together. And of course, she still wanted to be friends. I showed it to Pete and the LVT guys. One of the amtrack guys was a very talented calligrapher and, having become experts in the "Dear John" category, we decided to send her the:

DEAR JOHN OF THE MONTH AWARD
FOR THE MONTH OF JUNE 1969

DEAR DEBORAH,

CONGRATULATIONS! YOUR LETTER HAS BEEN SELECTED FROM THE MANY DEAR JOHNS SUBMITTED AS THE WINNER FOR THE MONTH OF JUNE 1969. YOUR LETTER WAS CHOSEN FOR ITS UNIQUE STYLE AND IT'S EXCELLENT COMPOSITION. YOUR LETTER WILL BE ENTERED WITH ALL OF THE OTHER MONTHLY WINNERS FOR THE:

"DEAR JOHN OF THE YEAR AWARD"

WE WISH YOU GOOD LUCK AND KEEP UP THE GOOD WORK.

SIGNED: (NAME, RANK, SERIAL NUMBER AND UNIT)

All the LVT guys, Pete and I signed it, and we sent it out on the next resupply helicopter.

Life settled down to a routine. Everyday we would get resupply, and then we would play cards with the LVT people, or hang out with Sergeant Lee and the supply section.

The amtrac people strung up a shade to the riverside of one of their machines, and put a couple of reclining lawn chairs under it to rest in during the day, and sometimes even sleep in during the night. One of the LVT guys and I decided to sleep outside in those chairs one night. In the middle of the night, a few Charlies crept to the other side of the river and decided to see if they could hit anyone in the dark.

They opened up with a machine gun and AK-47s. At the first round, I rolled off the recliner and crawled under the ramp and to the other side of the LVT where I was shielded. The amtrac guy I was sleeping by was still snoring away in his chair as green tracers buzzed overhead and ricocheted in the night. The guys inside the amtrac and I yelled at him, but despite our screaming and the gunfire, he continued his dreams. Some people can sleep through anything. I determined that something must be done or he was eventually going to get hit. The guys in the LVT couldn't leave their vehicle without exposing themselves; so I crawled back out under his chair, pushed up and tipped him out on the ground. He fell with a thud and that woke him up. He immediately realized that he was being shot at. We both scampered back to the safe side of the LVT. By now, the Koreans were returning fire and the VC/NVA left; or they were shot. Either way, they quit firing. No one was hit and the LVT guy was very grateful that I woke him up. No problem, I knew he would have done the same for me. We all laughed at how surprised he was when he was dumped from his chair. That was the only time we were shot at while by the river. That was also the last night I slept in those chairs.

The resupply had become so routine that the helicopters knew where the LZ was and one morning, they caught us by surprise. Pete and I were up by the Captain's bunker when we heard the CH-46s coming in with our daily resupply. Pete grabbed the radio to talk to the helicopters, and I had to get down to the LZ, about 100 yards away to guide them in. I ran as fast as I could to reach the LZ, and I arrived to see Long Size guiding the helicopter in. He had seen us do it hundreds of times, and he did it perfectly. When the resupply was over and the helicopters were gone, I went over to Long Size and patted him on the back, "Good Job Long Size!" He looked me in the eyes and spoke the first words of English I had ever heard him speak,

"Anglicoman Scott, my name not Long Size, my name Mister Chin."

Fighting back sudden and unexpected emotion, I put my hand on his shoulder and said, "Ok, Mister Chin, good job." Sergeant Lee told me later that, with his help, Mister Chin had been practicing that sentence for weeks. From that time forward, "Long Size" was only used in reference to cigars. Mister Chin became my right hand man, and we developed a wonderful friendship.

The LVT guys had a softball and bat that we borrowed one day, and Pete and I taught the Korean supply personnel how to play softball. I don't know that they learned anything, but we all had a great time, and we all laughed a lot.

On July 2nd, Battalion sent out, with the resupply, a FANG by the name of Vance Capehart for me to train. Pete went back to Battalion on the same helicopter to go on his special leave. Vance handed me a package. I opened it, and it was Don's .38 and shoulder holster. He had sent a note with it:

"Hey Wormo,
 Looks-ta-be I ain't gonna see ya before I go home but I'll write to ya a letter you'll get either when you come off leave (my special leave in 29 days) or maybe before. Take care of yourself man and on the pistol, I think you'll get more use out of it than I would.
Later, Don"

Then, he wrote down his home address. Gettle also sent a note out saying goodbye. His note had a dollar in it and said that now he only owed me $299. I had to step away to be by myself so that the FANG or the KMCs wouldn't see tears in my eyes. *And, I never saw Don or Gettle again.*

When I wrote to my parents and told them that I had lent Gettle that money, they thought I had lost $300. A few weeks later, they got a letter and $300 from Gettle.

While we were eating dinner one night, Sergeant Lee told me that I had been put in for the "INHUN" (Korean medal) by the Captain of 26th Company. I asked him why, and he said that the Captain thought I was a good man and that I deserved it. I felt honored to be nominated.

On the 12th of July, my twentieth birthday, the operation ended. I went back to Battalion, and Sergeant Lee went into Brigade to get ready to go home. We shook hands and said goodbye; we both may have blinked quite a bit. *I never saw Sergeant Lee again.*

Posing with Pete's .357 Revolver

POWs

On an operation, LVTs in background

Pete

Don checking in while we were building our bunker

With Don on an operation with bulldozers

Pete and me with Korean USO girl

KMC with POW

Back in the Field

Chapter 9
Special Leave

Almost as soon as I returned to Battalion, I received a letter from Debbie. She said that the "Dear John Award" had made her see how foolish she had been and that she had broken up with her old classmate. *At this point in time, it remained to be seen who the fool was.* She was now a freshman at Colorado State University in Fort Collins, Colorado. I thought about it for a few days, and then I wrote back to her. I was also writing to Peggy, an ex-classmate of Debbie and one of the girls I had dated on leave. I had received three letters from Debbie. She seemed to be making a sincere effort to mend fences with me. Peggy had been a faithful writer the whole time, and I felt like she liked me. My calendar was down to about twenty-four days before my special leave, and I could see a dilemma developing.

Because of all of the rotations, other than the current pilot on FO duty, USMC Lieutenant Nickols, we only had three guys at Battalion. Pete was on special leave and Scottie was on RnR. We also had to stick a guy out at 25th Company at night. So radio watch became six hours on and six hours off. Anglico HQ had better get some FANGS out here because I only had twenty more days till I left on my special leave.

Anglico Head Quarters sent out 35 year old Sergeant Baker to take Gettle's place. He was married and had a ten year old daughter. He was a pleasant enough fellow, and we got along well. Rex came out with Sergeant Baker. Rex had been in country for as long as I had, but he had been with a different detachment of Anglico. I liked Rex immediately, and he became one of my best friends. A few days later, a couple more guys joined us. One was a good natured nineteen-year old that was going prematurely bald. His name was Norman E. Wieser, and he asked us to call him "Bud." The other guy was a red-haired guy named Leonard Schaff. For obvious reasons, we called him "Red." Red had also been in country for awhile, but had been at Brigade until he came out to 5th Battalion. With the addition of three more people, radio watch became more tolerable. On our down time, we would play RISK, chess, or go down to the beach. Many times we were content with just having B.S. sessions.

The Lieutenant figured out that because we were part of MACV, we could go to the MACV base in Hoi An on Sundays for a lunch of steak and all the trimmings. It became a ritual. On Sundays, all of us but the guy on radio watch, would pile into Banard and go to Hoi An for lunch.

From Battalion, we took a right at the main road. We drove past 27th Company trail, LZ Dusty and 26th Company C.P. We came to a gate that marked the boundary of the Blue Dragon Brigade's control. The KMC guards waved us through. We paused at the intersection of a major road with signs pointing north and south. DaNang was to the north and Hoi An to the south. We turned left to go into Hoi An.

We made our visit a weekly trip, and we exchanged our dirty clothes for clean ones at a Vietnamese laundry. The Hoi An I saw was a dismal place. The homes, for the most part, were constructed of wood and whatever else was handy at the time. The residents didn't look much better. Whenever we had to stop for traffic, kids of all ages would swarm around Banard asking for gum or cigarettes. Apparently, the local laws concerning underage smoking were weak. It was a river town and the river was to the south. We drove past the ARVN compound by the river where Pete, Sergeant Lee and I were "shot at and missed." I wondered if the hand was still in the wire. We came to the nicer section of town with more stone buildings. The MACV detachment was inside a ten foot tall white walled compound. The two U.S. Army MPs who stood on guard at the gate recognized us and waved us in. Sarge always drove and the officer that was with us at the time, rode "shotgun." Up to five of us rode in the back.

It was a small base. I can't remember it very well, because in addition to steak and all the good things that go with steak, they also had a bar. One Sunday, it was busy and we had to wait quite awhile before we could eat. We waited in the bar and got badly soused.

Sarge had been in the Corps for fifteen years. He was jump qualified and always proudly wore his jump wings. At thirty-five years old, he was past his prime. But what Sarge had lost in fitness, he had gained in the ability to drink large quantities of liquor. I was never a big beer drinker, but mixed drinks, oh my. Sarge stood to make another toast to the Corps:

"I may get sh.tfaced and have to crawl out the door, but by God, I WILL crawl like a MARINE."

Then he threw up. "Well," I thought, "Sarge is done now." He wiped his mouth off on his sleeve and raised his glass,

"To the Corps!" and finished his drink. You gotta drink to the Corps. We ate our steaks with our hands. Crazy; "You never act like that at home" my Mother would have said. I am sure that our behavior raised some eyebrows, but no one ever said anything to us. It did seem though, that we didn't have to wait as long to go through the chow line the next Sunday. We never forgot to take home a big helping of everything for the guy on radio watch.

The Koreans had their own version of a USO show. We called in a CH-46 one day that had a whole troop of Korean USO performers, mostly young cute girls. They put on a show for the Korean Marines on the stage outside of our door. We sat on top of Banard and our bunker while we watched. The Koreans trucked my old 26th Company in for the show, and I looked up my old Korean friends.

We Americans understood very little of the show, but the Koreans loved it and clapped and cheered like it was the greatest thing. After the show, Rex and I went down to where the Korean officers were having a picnic with the performers, and we were invited to join them for lunch. Lunch was a fancy version of what we ate with the Koreans everyday. As always, the menu was rice, kimchi and soup, but they went all out and had a few extra Korean delicacies like dried squid and lots of beer. We posed for photos with the Korean show girls, sometimes at our request, sometimes at theirs.

"Guns," our pig always stayed close to our bunker. She seemed to sense that if she strayed too far from us she might end up in a soup. She was like a watch dog, and she did not like most of the Korean Marines. One day, one of the Korean officers came to our hooch and asked us to please not let our pig chase his men. We promised that we would do our best to control her.

Just as I was getting ready to go on special leave, our home was in the process of being remodeled. The Koreans built us a 16' X 30' hooch. The top half of the long walls had screens to provide for air circulation. They put a partition across a third of it and made it the sleeping quarters for the officer attached to us. The other two thirds were our new sleeping quarters. We still only had cots to sleep on, but we enjoyed our new room. *I fondly remember and miss going to sleep to the sound of the waves lapping on the beach about thirty yards away.*

Once in awhile, the Koreans would bring us ice (Korean word, "aut-om") and for a little while, we had cold beer and cold water. One day we were going to dump the old water from the metal cooler and were shocked to see a dead mouse floating in it. Apparently, the mouse was in some of the ice the Koreans brought us. We all kinda gagged, but there wasn't much that could be done about it now. Other than that incident, life was becoming easy. We had a real coffee pot and no longer had to rely on instant coffee to help us stay awake during our radio watch. We also had Pete's portable TV and our stereo with a nice selection of reel to reel tapes. Between the TV, music, board and card games, we had plenty to keep us entertained. And of course, we spent a lot of time at the beach swimming and body surfing.

One morning a Korean Lieutenant came over and told us that the compound was getting a seventy foot tower. The Koreans had laid concrete foundations for the four tower legs. I stood by on the radio as a sky-crane helicopter approached from the north with the tower dangling underneath. I was on the radio and Pete guided the helicopter into position. As the helicopter started to lower the tower, the Koreans rushed up and attached ropes to the tower legs to help guide it onto the concrete bases. There must have been thirty Koreans helping guide the tower down. Korean officers and NCOs were trying to shout orders above the noise of the sky-crane. I told the helicopter to slowly lower it and all of a sudden, one of the KMC privates started screaming. We had lowered in onto his foot. I told the helicopter to pick up the tower, and the Korean was released. We eventually got the tower attached to the base and the sky-crane unhooked and left. We called in a medivac for the Korean with the smashed foot.

I remember that when Pete and I told the rest of the Anglico guys about the Korean having his foot smashed, all the old guys laughed. The new guys looked a little shocked. A smashed foot seemed like a funny thing compared to most of the other wounds we had seen. I am not laughing now. That guy probably lost his foot and was condemned to be crippled for the rest of his life.

The tower was an awesome observation platform. We used it to call in air strikes on areas that we received fire from and for general observation. One day, after I had called in an air strike, I started the long climb down the almost vertical seventy foot ladder. The Prick 25 tended to make me top heavy, and I had to hold on tight to the ladder to make sure I would not topple over backwards and fall. I did not have my helmet on, and I was concentrating on getting down safely, when all of a sudden, something heavy hit me on my head. Stunned, my knees buckled and I almost lost my grip. I locked my knees and wrapped my arms around the ladder and held on as my vision cleared. A Korean Private had started down after me and as he tilted his head up, his helmet had fallen off and dropped twenty-five feet, whacking me on the head. I recovered from the blow and finished my descent. The Korean apologized and since no permanent harm had been done, I accepted his apology. After all of the booby traps and being shot at too many times to count, that would have been a less than heroic way to die.

I was busy getting my uniforms ready for special leave. I had my Lance Corporal stripes sewn on my summer uniform and had purchased the ribbons I had been awarded. After much work, my dress shoes had a nice spit shine. I informed my parents that I would probably be home about the 12th or 13th of August. Debbie and I had resumed a hot correspondence, and I had promised her that she and a friend of mine, Larry, could come to the airport to pick me up. Peggy had written and asked me to call her, day or night, as soon as I landed in California so she could pick me up in Denver. My parents were also expecting to pick me up. I chose Debbie.

I had ruled out my parents picking me up because I was twenty years old, and I was looking forward to a little romance. That narrowed my choice down to Debbie or Peggy. There are decisions that people make in their life which are more important than they seem at the time. I decided to have Debbie pick me up as opposed to Peggy. I am not sure why. Peggy was cute and had been very nice to me. I am sure that had I decided to have Peggy pick me up, my life would have taken a very different course. What is: is.

We had received a new pilot by the name of Captain Bodkin. He was a nice person, and we had become good friends and chess opponents. Red was also a very good chess player and at every opportunity, two of us played while the third watched. They were both much better than me and I learned a lot. I had learned how the pieces moved when I was about twelve. I however, did not know how to "play" chess. Captain Bodkin explained the philosophy of chess, and I learned to appreciate the strategy involved. I had to go out to 27th Company for a week while their company was on an operation. While I was out there, Captain Bodkin and I played chess every night on an unused radio frequency. If the enemy had been listening, I am sure that the chess notations confused them, "Roger one four, this is Charlie, king's bishop four to queen's rook four, check." When it came time for me to go home on special leave, I had learned enough that I had started to win a few games

On or about August 3rd, I left Battalion for my long trip to go home for thirty days. I went from Battalion to Brigade, then to DaNang. From there I caught a C-47 to Saigon. I left Saigon on a Freedom bird (commercial airliner). Eventually, I landed at Stapleton International Airport in Denver about 10:00 AM one morning in early August, 1969. I met Larry first; he said Debbie was here somewhere and was looking for me. Debbie and I saw each other about the same time. We embraced as though we were long lost lovers.

My Mom was pretty upset that I didn't let them pick me up. *She had a right to be upset.*

Debbie was a dance major at Colorado State University in Ft. Collins, and I accompanied her to all of her classes. One of her classes required that she go golfing. I went golfing with her on a small course between Ft. Collins and Loveland. It is fortunate my MOS was not artillery. I hit a horse.

I attended one of her classes in which they started discussing Nixon's recent decision to invade Cambodia. An Air Force ROTC student stood up and explained that ground troops were not necessary, and that air power could accomplish the mission of interdicting the Ho Chi Mien Trail. I had heard just about enough bull sh.t and stated so quite loudly: "BULL SH*T!" The room was silent. The ROTC student asked what I had said. I repeated my first statement. Then I told him, "Air power is an awesome weapon, but it cannot find the enemy or destroy him." The student wanted to know what made me an authority. I told him that I was a Marine forward observer that was in Vietnam less than a month ago, and that I would be back there within the month. I also informed them that I approved of the decision to invade Cambodia and why. I am quite certain that I wasted my breath.

I saw a number of war protesters while I was with Debbie at CSU. While I was in Vietnam, we had many B.S. sessions concerning the war and how to win it. We were chomping at the bit to invade North Vietnam, to hell with the political reaction. We were in favor of any tactic that would help us win. The Invasion of Cambodia made good sense to us, and we all approved. In addition to a direct invasion of North Vietnam, there were many other proposals. Don had been in favor of the nuclear option. "Nuke em. If China or Russia say anything, nuke em." Another proposed solution was: "Put all the good Vietnamese on a boat, sink the place, then, sink the boat."

I have mixed opinions of the war protesters. While debating a number of protesters, I found that many did not have a clear understanding of the Vietnam War. I think about half of the protesters understood the war and had legitimate arguments. The other half protested because it was the "cool thing to do". I have no problem with those that opposed the war on moral grounds. In fact, I salute you. My opinion drops significantly if someone protested because it was cool or to save their own skin. My criterion for "Victory" was simple. If South Vietnam could exist as a free, democratic country, we have a "VICTORY!" That opinion was reinforced by the fact that I was serving with a people that had battled for their freedom not twenty years ago and won. If South Vietnam turned out as well as South Korea, we win.

I spent a lot of my special leave with Debbie. It seemed that I had forgotten all of the "Dear John" letters, the last one less than two months ago. I was smitten, and I was sure that we were in love and were going to be together forever. So I bought her an engagement ring, and we set the date for our wedding on July 18, 1970, a few months after I came home from Vietnam.

The Korean word for "crazy" is "Ko-dee-bee-essa." The Korean word for "foolish man" is "jō da." Sergeant Lee would have said, "Anglicoman Scott, Ko-dee-bee-essa jo da." My mother didn't use those exact words, but she made it clear that she had her doubts concerning my engagement. She finally conceded that if Debbie could wait for me for seven more months while I was in Vietnam, maybe it would work.

I did spend some time with my family. One day, Sweet Ma prepared a big dinner with many of my extended family as well as Debbie and her family in attendance. Mom was an antique dealer, and she had a sideboard in the dinning room that was full of antique dishes. We were all sitting at the large dining room table, and the conversation had stopped so that my Grandfather could say the blessing. It was quiet except for my Grandfather's soft prayer and the rattling and clinking of those antique dishes. After the "Amen," all of us opened our eyes and silently stared in wonder at the dishes on the sideboard as they continued to shake and rattle. The antique chandelier over the table seemed to be swaying gently. We had never had an earthquake. Debbie put her hand on my leg, and my bouncing leg and the clinking ceased. *I still have that nervous bounce at times.*

Debbie and my parents took me to the airport on September 15th. It was the first time I felt really bad about leaving. It was a tearful goodbye.

From Stapleton, I went to California, then to Anchorage, Alaska. I stayed in Alaska for a couple of hours, then flew to Japan. From there I flew to Okinawa.

I had to stay in Okinawa until the 19th. Okinawa had a reputation of being a den of thieves. I slept in a transit barracks, and I had put my wallet under my pillow to protect it. The thief was good. The next morning, my empty wallet lay on my chest. I had no money. I ate in the mess hall, and for the most part, I didn't need money, but by now I had developed a nicotine habit and I ran out of cigarettes. *Interesting note: During the 19 months I was with the Koreans, I was not, nor did I hear of anyone else being, the victim of theft.*

On the morning of the 19th, I went to the airport terminal, and I sat down by another Marine Lance Corporal who was also on his way back to Vietnam. We were in our summer uniforms, and he wore a large number of ribbons.

One was the "Purple Heart" ribbon, which indicated that he had been wounded in action. We had to wait quite a while for our flights, and we started visiting.

I asked him for a cigarette. We hit if off and I enjoyed our visit. I told him how I had lost all of my money, but other than the need for tobacco, I didn't need money. I asked him about the "Purple Heart," and he told me how he had been wounded. He was a modest person, but his ribbons, which included the "Bronze Star with a 'V' for Valor," spoke highly of him. My flight to Saigon was boarding, and I shook his hand goodbye. He opened his wallet and he had twenty dollars. He gave me a ten as well as half of his cigarettes. I thanked him and boarded the plane.

This act of kindness touched me deeply. I had only known him for a couple of hours, and he gave me half of his stuff. I have a philosophy. Had I never been a victim of a low life stealing my money, I would never have realized how good a person that Lance Corporal was. I have long since forgotten his name, but never his generosity. I pray that he made it home.

How can one recognize good times if one has never experienced bad times? You need a basis for comparison.

I was back at 5th Battalion by the 22nd of September. I started counting the days until I could go home again.

Bringing in the top of the tower

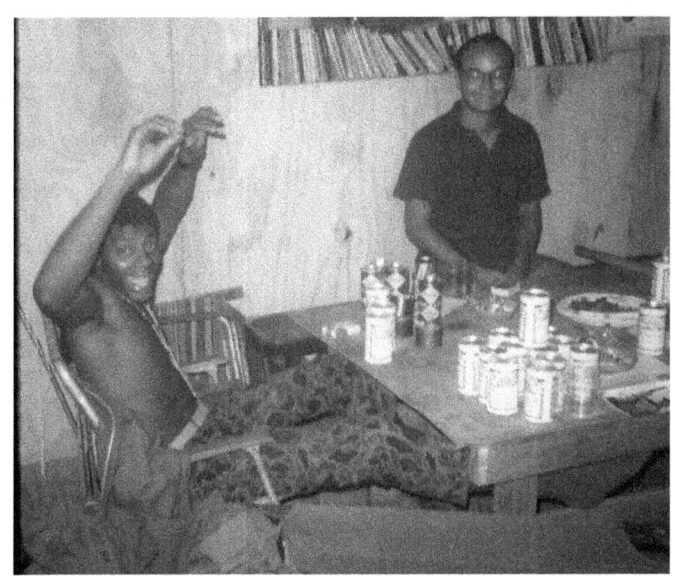

Scottie and Budwieser

Special Leave

Red, Pete and Rex

Chapter 10
Back to the War

When I got back to 5th Battalion, I learned from Sarge that everyone else was on a big operation, "Operation Victory Dragon XV" on Barrier Island.

I went into our new sleeping quarters and was amazed that we had bunk beds; so much better than cots. I asked Sarge where they came from. He told me that while I was on special leave, they (Sarge, Rex, Red, Budweiser and Pete) went to the Air Force base in DaNang. Sarge knew someone there, and they had a nice meal, and after dinner they were put up in a large barracks. They were the only people assigned to the large room. Sarge decided that the bunks would serve us better at home than sitting in an empty barracks. So they all took a nap. Then, in the middle of the night, they got up and dismantled four of the bunk beds and loaded them up in the back of Banard. They made the dark (and dangerous) drive home. *Recently, Rex told me that they were lying on top of the mattresses and expected to run into bad guys laying mines on Hwy 1. No one was out, good guys or bad guys, and they all breathed a sigh of relief when the Korean guards waved them into 5th Battalion's C.P.*

I went out the next day to join Captain Bodkin and Red at Battalion Forward.

Sarge drove me to LZ Dusty where Dusty informed me which helicopters were going to 5th Battalion forward. I ran over and hopped on a CH-46 which was packed with supplies. We flew south and landed on a grassy area by a river. I ran off the ramp of the helicopter and waved at Red, who had landed the resupply. Red and Captain Bodkin were glad to see me as they had to maintain a 24 hour radio watch which was always hard on two people. Captain Bodkin caught me up on what had happened while I was on leave.

He told me that at about 8:00 AM on the 12th of September 5th, Battalion made a combat amphibious assault on the north beach of Barrier Island. The assault was largely unopposed. A large part of the Blue Dragon Brigade's assets were involved in this operation as well as a large U.S. Marine contingent.

I regretted then, and I still regret to this day, that I missed that amphibious assault; the old "Once a Marine, always a Marine." Had I know we were going to do an amphibious assault, I would have tried to postpone my leave.

This was the first operation I had been on with Battalion HQ. The position looked much like a company's position, but it was purely defensive. It was a large operation with lots of action. The available helicopter support was taxed to keep up with the demands of the operation. Medivacs, emergency resupply and troop lifts all vied for priority.

I took the six to midnight radio watch that night while Red and Captain Bodkin slept in our small two man bunker. I woke Red at midnight, and he relieved me of the watch, and I went to sleep. I was awakened by machine gun fire. Captain Bodkin and Red were crouched behind the bunker as I crawled out. In the night sky, fifty yards to our north, green (bad guy) tracers were crisscrossing the red (good guys) tracers going the other way. I was still groggy from just having wakened, and I was certain that Captain Bodkin and Red were in danger. I tried to convince them that they were in peril and that they had to move. Red argued that they were in a safe position here and that moving anywhere could be deadly. I finally woke up enough to realize that he was right.

I have thought a lot about that night. I think that I reacted the way I did because I had subconsciously flashed back to the night I was sleeping by the LVT. The last time I was awakened by green tracers, they were bouncing off the side of the amtrac and someone else was in danger. Or, maybe it was because I had been out of country for a month, and I had lost my edge. Or, it just may be that in the span of a week, it is hard to adjust from "making out" in my parent's station wagon to taking cover behind a bunker. Whatever it was, it bothered me.

The firing eventually died out, and I went back to sleep so I could relieve Red at 0600 the next morning.

The next day was a busy one, with all the companies calling in lots of medivacs, air strikes and resupply. The companies requested all support through us, and then we relayed to Brigade and helped coordinate the air support. Rex was with 27th Company, and he called in that morning with a request for helicopters to evacuate the large number of prisoners his company had captured. I told Rex that I would forward the request, but that there were lots of emergency medivacs, troop lifts and emergency resupply missions. Evacuating prisoners was pretty low on the priority list.

An hour later, he called back in and said that his Korean Captain was becoming impatient because his company could not move until the large number of prisoners was gone. I told Rex that I understood the situation, and that I would relay that information to Brigade.

One and a half hours later, Rex checked in. I told him that we should soon have his helicopters to evacuate the prisoners. He said, "Oh, that's ok, we don't have any prisoners now." I asked him to repeat his last transmission. He said, "Roger Scorcher One Four, I say again, we don't have any prisoners now, and we are sweeping to the south." I didn't ask any more questions.

The operation ended a week later, and we were helilifted back to LZ Dusty. Helicopter evacuations from the field were always a tricky business. We never had enough helicopters to take the entire force out at once, and we went out in stages on two CH-46s. I had to land the helicopters on their return trip, and we were the last ones on the last sortie to get on the helicopter. It was always a little scary after the next to the last group left. Now there were only about thirty KMC and Red and I. I thought, "Sure hope Charlie does not decide to attack now." We had two Huey gunships flying around us to make sure that we had immediate support should we need it. If there were any NVA/VC in the surrounding woods, they were probably happy to see us leave, and we took no fire.

Barrier Island was a big operation, and we were all glad to be home again. Rex came in from 27th Company for awhile, and we quickly adjusted to radio watch and the good life at Battalion.

One night, I was on radio watch in the TOC. It was 0200 on a quiet night, and I was busy writing letters when the Korean Lieutenant on duty came over and told me that a USMC patrol had gotten lost and was in our (the Korean) area of operations. We went over to the large table map, and he pointed out the location of a KMC ambush team and the location of the lost USMC patrol. I told him that I would call Brigade and find out what was going on. I told Brigade (Past One Four) that there was a lost USMC patrol in our area. Brigade told me that he would check on it. "Past One Four" called me a few minutes later and told me that he had contacted the USMC unit to the north of us, and that they had no USMC units at the coordinates in question.

I went back to the Korean Lieutenant and told him, "USMC say they have no one at that location." He insisted that there was a USMC patrol because his ambush team has a visual. I called Brigade back and asked him to check again as the Koreans were quite sure. He checked again, and told me that the USMC insisted that no one was lost.

I relayed that information to the KMC Lieutenant. He shook his head and pointed to the map. "Ok," putting his finger on the map, "this is USMC; I will fire mortars here and here and here and here". He intended to fire mortars all around the patrol, but at a distance where it would do no harm. I smiled and told him to do it. Shortly after that, I could hear the mortars firing.

A few minutes went by. Then, this time, "Past One Four" called me. A USMC patrol had called in, and they had mortars dropping in a 360 degree circle around them. They were lost. The Korean Lieutenant and I smiled. We stopped firing the mortars, and the USMC patrol went back to their own area. Some USMC NCO probably got chewed out for getting lost.

In early November, I joined Pete at 26th Company. Lieutenant Kim, Moon and Mr. Chin were excited to see me, and we exchanged greetings. We were going on an operation to clear woods and destroy enemy bunkers and tunnels. We were accompanied by two LVTs and two bulldozers.

One of the LVTs was outfitted with a rocket propelled demolition charge mounted on top of the LVT. I cannot explain the way it worked. I can describe the effect. The LVT fired a rocket propelled C-4 demolition charge (C-4 is a highly explosive clay-like substance). I do not know how big the charge was, but it must have been hundreds of pounds. As the rocket screamed away from the LVT, it trailed an explosive cord back to the amtrack. The cord provided the operator with the means to detonate the charge after it had landed. The mission was to destroy heavily wooded areas. When the operator detonated the charge, it created a tremendous explosion that destroyed all the trees within approximately fifty yards.

It was hot (*unless it was raining, it was always hot*), and we had entered a heavily wooded area. We halted to take a break. I dropped my radio, rifle and helmet and had just sat down with my back against a tree, when I heard the LVT fire its rocket propelled charge. The rocket went over the tree I was leaning against and with a loud "whump", landed thirty yards beyond me. The cord lay five feet in front of me. The area was crawling with Koreans and if that charge went off, it was gonna kill a bunch of them and probably me. I jumped to my feet and following the cord, I ran as hard as I could to stop the LVT from detonating the charge. I saw the LVT as I ran out of the woods and ran toward it waving and screaming. When I reached the LVT, they assured me that they knew the charge went off course, and they had no intention of detonating the charge. It turned out that I had run for naught; but for a little bit, it looked pretty scary. I walked back to the tree where my rifle, helmet and radio lay.

While talking to Anglicoman Joe Medina recently, he told me that the above mentioned LVT had an accident while they were with his company. Joe said the base of the LVT was blown half-a-foot into the ground. Joe and his counterpart called in a routine medivac for the six crew members. Joe said they gathered about ten pounds of human remains in a poncho to put on the helicopter.

The next morning, the Korean Captain requested an air strike on a wood line on the far side of a fifty foot wide stream. Pete and I crawled to a little sandy ridge about ten yards from the stream. We switched to the frequency of the spotter plane and made radio contact. When he requested a smoke, we tossed a yellow one about five feet from us. To our surprise, the spotter marked the target area, about 100 yards across the stream, with another yellow smoke. Pete called the spotter and advised him that we also had a yellow smoke, and we didn't want the jets to be confused. He assured us that the jets understood which side of the stream to drop their ordnance.

They screamed in low over our smoke and made a wide turn to come in on the target. They came in one at a time. Pete and I were pretty close to the target, and we lay down behind the small sand ridge to watch the bombing run. The first F-4 dropped double canisters of napalm. At only 100+ yards, the napalm was impressive and would have made an awesome photo. I grabbed my camera and knelt on the sand hill to catch the next run. We figured we could expose ourselves a little because if there was someone over there, they had more to worry about than us as the second jet came in. I focused on the target area and waited. I saw the jet streak across my camera view finder and saw his ordnance fall away. They were not canisters of napalm but two 250 lb. snake-eye bombs. Pete and I dove behind the sand ridge as the bombs exploded and sent shrapnel into and over the sand that we were hiding behind. I missed the photo.

We crossed the stream with the company and found that one of the casualties was, what I believed to be, a jaguar. He had beautiful fur but was badly torn up. *War is hard on all living things that have the misfortune to be in it's path.*

A couple of days later, after a morning of sweeping, we stopped for a break in a bushy area. I helped Pete take the radio off, and we sat on a fallen tree. To our back was a ten foot tall bush that we couldn't see through. We had been sitting there about five minutes when some Koreans started shouting in the thick foliage behind us. The bush came alive with gunfire and shouting. Pete and I fell down behind the log and took cover at the first blast of gunfire. We had our weapons ready, but because some of the fire was coming out of the area in our direction, we felt like we dare not peek over the log. A couple of grenades went off, and after a few more shots, the firing died out, and we heard Koreans talking and approaching. Pete and I got to our feet and with weapons ready, cautiously walked around the bush. A couple of the Koreans were kicking the four badly mangled bodies on the ground to make sure they were dead. Three or four other KMC were standing cover. Pete and I stood and looked at the bodies. It took a while before I realized that one of them was a young girl. She may have been pretty a couple of minutes ago. I noticed that one of the dead was in a NVA uniform with a star NVA belt buckle. His web belt was almost cut in two by some of the grenade shrapnel. I had given Don Webber my NVA buckle when he went home, and I decided that I needed another one. I took my bayonet out of the sheath and cut the web belt where the grenade shrapnel had done most the work. I took the dead soldiers web belt and buckle over to a flooded bomb crater and cut the belt off the buckle. I sat on my haunches and washed the flesh and blood off the buckle and put it in my shirt pocket.

We swept every day, and the LVTs and two bulldozers continued the process of tearing up the woods.

One day, during one of those sweeps, we had three KMC emergency medivacs from a booby trap. We called it in, but it was taking a long time for the helicopters to arrive. The Koreans were becoming anxious, and we called "Past One Four" and asked what the problem was. He advised us that there were lots of medivacs going on right now, and that he would try to hurry our request along.

While we waited, we noticed a small two-man U.S. Army helicopter buzzing around our area. He came on our frequency and asked us if he could help. I thanked him, but advised him that we had three emergency medivacs, and that he had no room on that little helicopter.

Without a zone brief or any further conversation, he landed. One of the Army guys jumped out and helped us load a wounded Korean in his seat. The little chopper took off for the hospital in DaNang. Soon he was back for another wounded Korean. One at a time, he carried out all three of our wounded to the hospital. He came back for his co-pilot and left. I was very impressed with that U.S. Army pilot and his little helicopter. He probably saved some lives that day. I called "Past One Four" and cancelled our medivac request.

We came off the operation on the 20th of November, and I went back to Battalion for a few days. When I arrived, Sarge called me to the side. He told me in a low voice that Pete and I had made Corporal. I said "Cool. Why are we whispering?" He explained that no one knew about it yet, and I was not supposed to know because the Major wanted to surprise me and pin my stripes on. "Oh, ok, no problem." I asked, "How much more money do I get?" He smiled and said, "About fifty dollars more a month!" I thought about it for a little bit, and then I told him, "I'm proud to be a Corporal in the Marines." He corrected me, "You are not a 'Corporal in the Marines'; you are a 'Corporal of Marines.'" There is a subtle but significant difference.

We all liked and enjoyed being with Captain Bodkin, and we had talked him into spending another 100 days with us. He agreed to do so, but he had to fly so many hours a month to collect his flight pay. He flew an A-6 Intruder, an all weather attack jet, and swore by them. He scorned the F-4 Phantom as a fuel-hog clumsy beast. I liked any and all air support.

I had a lot of packages and letters waiting for me when I came in. Many of them were from Debbie. She more than made up for all the other girls that had stopped writing to me. She was being a good fiancée. I had lost my "gung ho" attitude, and told Sarge that I would do anything he asked me to do, but that I was not going to volunteer any more. He assured me that he understood and that he would not order me to do anything more than he had to.

A couple of days later, we went into Brigade and the Major pinned my Corporal stripes on my collar. Three days later, Sarge asked me to go back out to 26th Company. I packed my gear and joined Pete with 26th Company for another operation.

Running an air strike

My NVA belt buckle

Riding a LVT coming in off an operation

Chapter 11
The Church

We took trucks from 26th Company to LZ Dusty. There we boarded two CH-46s. We flew to the west of Hoi An, and we were dropped off in a large clear area. Again, we had to be shuttled in as we only had two helicopters assigned to the lift. Pete and I were on the first helicopter in so we could direct the air support if it was needed. We packed those two helicopters with about 25 or 30 people each. On landing, the Koreans moved to secure the LZ. I established radio contact with the pair of Huey Cobras flying cover that were ready to suppress any incoming fire. *The Cobra was a fairly new attack helicopter that resembled a shark. It was armed with a mini-gun and/or a 20mm cannon and also carried rockets. It was, in a word, nasty.* The Company arrived without taking fire.

Pete and I found the HQ group, and after the Company had deployed in a wide attack formation, we moved toward a large woods to the southwest. We entered the woods without taking fire, and we continued our advance through the heavy underbrush. To keep my tape antenna from getting caught in the low branches, I pulled it down over my shoulder and tucked it in a web loop on my flak jacket. Our visibility was limited, and we could only see about thirty or forty feet in any direction.

We had only been moving in the woods for a short time when a large firefight erupted in my section of the line. The loud cracks of the AK-47s indicated that they were close. As I heard the rounds buzzing nearby and hitting the trees, I looked for the nearest cover. Ten feet in front of me was a small foot and a half embankment along a small stream. I dove face down behind the embankment and hugged the ground as the incoming rounds whizzed over my prone body.

I made myself as flat as I could and cursed the radio on my back that made me stick up a little higher. I turned my head to the left to see if I could see Pete or any of the KMC. I gasped as my eyes focused on a two foot snake lying face to face with me about five inches away from my nose. *During staging, they had told us that "There are one thousand species of snakes in Vietnam. Nine hundred and ninety-nine of those species are poisonous. The other one eats you whole."* The good news was, this was not the one that could eat me whole.

On the ranch, rattlesnakes are something to be concerned about. From the first time I was old enough to go outside by myself, the last thing my parents said as I went out the door was: "Watch out for snakes!" Had they warned me everyday to: "Watch out for butterflies and snakes!" I would probably hate and fear butterflies as much as I do snakes.

As I lay by the snake and watched him flicking his tongue at me, I thought of my options: "He might bite me, but if I expose myself in the least, I'll probably be shot." I chose the snake, and we lay together behind that small embankment. I whispered to the snake, "Ok snake, I won't bother you if you don't bother me." Apparently, we had a truce, and after a bit of time, he slithered away. As I watched him leave, I had an involuntary shudder. I was, however, a little envious of how low he could lay on the ground.

The firefight ended, and we had a few casualties.

There was an opening in the woods just beyond the stream. The Koreans moved into the next tree line fifty yards away. We were still taking sporadic sniper fire when we called in the zone brief to Past One Four. After we called it in, we had a lot of work to do before the helicopters came. The zone was considered "hot," and we knew that the helicopters would want permission to fire. While Pete coordinated with Lieutenant Kim to determine exactly where all of the friendlies were, I had our map out and was determining exactly where we were. One of the landmarks I took a compass bearing on to determine our position was a large solitaire rocky mountain to the southwest. It loomed over the trees and was the highest point for miles around. After we had all the friendly positions marked on the map, we knew where we could give the helicopters clearance to fire.

The CH-46 came escorted by two Huey gunships. We gave them the zone brief and told the gunships where they were cleared to fire. And fire they did. They pretty well worked over the area beyond the Korean forward line. We didn't take any incoming, and the medivac was over in a couple of minutes.

After the medivac, we continued sweeping southwest. Whenever we crossed an opening in the woods, we could see the mountain looming ever higher. After a long hot walk, we finally exited the woods and moved across a clearing to the base of the mountain where we set up camp for the night. Four hundred yards to the west of our position was a dark foreboding forest. A glance at the map confirmed that it was a large forest. When we dug in that night, the Koreans placed most of their thirty caliber machine guns and claymore mines facing west.

Pete and I expected that we might have to call in a "Spooky" that night, so we had a long sit-down talk with Lieutenant Kim over the map. We had to make sure we knew where everyone was.

Late that night, we were attacked from that wood line. And, as expected, the Captain asked for "Spooky." We requested the gunship from Brigade and within thirty minutes, we made radio contact with Spooky. He flew over the forest and dropped a flare. Our position was easy to mark, and on the next pass, he opened fire. Spooky, as always, seemed to have the last word in a firefight, and we took no more fire from the tree line that night.

I had determined that if I was under attack there is no place I would rather be than inside a KMC position. Whenever we stopped for the night, everyone, with the exception of the officers, started digging. In a matter of hours, they could turn a patch of open ground into a nasty entrenched position. They were a digging people. I am sure that we suffered fewer casualties because of that extra protection.

The next morning, we remained where we were and Pete and I called in a resupply mission. Because we were air lifted in, we didn't have the LVTs and their cargo capacity to haul supplies. We had to rely on air resupply to keep us in ammo, food and water. We had consumed much of what we had yesterday and last night. We landed the two CH-46s while two Hueys shot up the forest. Helicopters don't like to stay around any longer than necessary when flying into a zone that has been recently fired upon. The Koreans were extremely efficient at unloading the large nets under the helicopters full of the cargo of ammo, k-rations, rice and water. In less than a minute, the helicopters were emptied, and they rose and tilted forward as they turned away from the forest.

We remained at the base of that mountain until about 3:00 that afternoon. Then, much to our dismay, Lieutenant Kim informed Pete and me that we had received orders to climb to the top of the mountain. It was hot, and that mountain looked hard. It was treeless, rocky and seemed to go straight up. We had just been resupplied, and the Koreans had to load up with all of the extra ammo boxes, water, k-rat cases and bags of rice. Pete helped me put the radio on as I stood and stared at my next challenge.

It was not straight up, but we were on all fours much of the time as we clawed our way up the steep incline. It tested my strength and endurance more than they had ever been tested. I had to remind myself that I was a U.S. Marine, and I could not let the KMC outdo me. I paused for a breather, sat down on a large rock and took a long drink of warm iodine tainted water. As I screwed the cap back onto the canteen, I looked around at my Korean comrades. I had the radio and it was heavy, but the KMC were carrying boxes of ammo, k-rations and bags of rice. I even saw a couple of Korean privates in the HQ group pulling a large ice cooler up behind them. I thought, "What in the world is in that cooler?"

We finally reached the top, which was just as ugly and barren as the sides had been. The summit was not a large area, and the company had a hard time deploying up there, so many of the KMC remained on the upper slopes. The whole company fell to the ground in exhaustion. I dropped my radio and was flat on my back gasping for air. I looked to

The Church

my side, and I could see that everyone, including the Captain, was as whipped as I was.

After a few minutes, I started to recover and sat up. I saw the Captain sit up, and he called over the two guys that had been lugging that cooler up the mountain. They hopped up and carried their cooler over to the Captain. He gave them an order, and they opened up the lid, pulled out a can of beer and handed it to him. He then gave another order, and one of the KMC pulled out two beers and ran over and gave Pete and I each an ice-cold beer. I told him, "Com hom som D da," "Thank you very much," in Korean. He nodded and ran back to his cooler. Pete and I raised our beers in salute to the Captain. *In a perfect world, those two Korean Privates should have each gotten a cold beer for their efforts. I doubt it happened. If I was perfect, I would have given them mine.* Never had a cold beer tasted so good.

Pete and I found a spot where we planned on staying that night. There were very few flat areas on the summit. We found the best area we could, but we had to prop our feet against some rocks to keep from sliding back down the steep slope. We sat down and looked at the world below us.

The mountain was what the military refer to as "The Commanding Position." We had a bird's-eye view of everything within miles. To the north-north-east we could see "Monkey Mountain" just south of DaNang. There were air strikes in progress that had nothing to do with us, and we just enjoyed the view. That large dark forest lay to the northwest of us.

We didn't dig in that night as it was all rock. Pete and I were eating our supper of rice, soup and kimchi when

Lieutenant Kim came over and explained what the plan was.

Tomorrow morning, the Korean Artillery was going to bombard that dark forest for awhile. Then, the artillery would cease fire at 0900 for a B-52 strike. After the B-52 strike, a spotter plane would direct air strikes on targets of opportunity. Then we would climb down this mountain and enter that forest. Sounded like a plan. This was the first B-52 strike I would see close up and I was excited.

It was hard to sleep that night. We slept fully clothed underneath the stars on hard jagged rocks. Every now and then, I felt like I started to lose my footing, and I jerked awake. It was about 10:00 that night when we were awakened by Spooky working out in the distance. He was close enough that we could just hear his mini-guns "buzz" as they fired.

As we watched, we saw that he was taking ground fire on each circle. We noticed that the enemy would wait until Spooky had flown over him, then he would open up with a machine gun. We could see his tracers reaching up toward the unsuspecting gunship. We found Spooky's frequency and gave him a call on the radio and advised him that someone was shooting at him. He seemed excited and wanted a fix on the enemy machine gun. We gave him our position and then gave him a compass bearing from our position to the machine gun. Another Anglicoman from a different position gave Spooky his bearing to the target. The Spooky navigator then drew a line from our position and from the other position. Where those lines intersected was the location of the bad guy machine gun. On the next pass, Spooky opened up on those coordinates. The offending machine gun ceased firing. It took a lot of guts, or a really bad judgment call, to shoot at Spooky.

After Spooky left, Pete and I tried to get some rest. I awoke at dawn after a fitful sleep. I sat up and opened a can of c-rat peaches for breakfast. Then I made a can of c-rat instant coffee in the peach can. I built a little platform out of the rocks to hold my can of iodine water and put a heat tablet under the can and lit it. Soon, I had hot water for instant coffee with powdered cream and sugar with only a slight iodine aftertaste. It is amazing how satisfying a little victory like making coffee can be. I sipped my coffee and nibbled on a c-rat chocolate disk sandwiched between two crackers and watched the day come to life.

After we did our business off the side of the bald mountain, we found the Korean Captain and Lieutenant Kim. We sat down by them to watch the show.

Sure enough, at precisely 0800, the Korean Artillery Battalion opened up on the "enchanted forest". I had never been subjected to enemy artillery as many of my brother Marines had been. Just having it scream over my head and explode with a sharp crack over and in the woods in front of me was bad enough. It took a few rounds before I was able to control my instinct to duck.

From our mountain viewpoint, we had great seats to watch good ol' firepower. They were firing 105mm and maybe a few 155mm shells. Most were air-bursts. I understood why people went mad under an artillery barrage. At about 0840, the artillery abruptly stopped firing. As the dust settled, smoke was drifting skyward from a dozen small fires. Pete looked at his watch and turned to me, "The B-52 strike is next."

We strained our eyes and ears to search for the B-52s. We had no control over this strike since it was controlled by radio beacons. I thought I saw the contrails just as the forest seemed to erupt like an ocean wave of fire and dirt. The explosions engulfed all in its path, and the path was wide. The ground shook and the rolling thunder was terrifying. Then it was over. The fires in the forest were larger and more numerous than before, adding their smoke to the otherwise clear day.

We put on our gear and started down the mountain as a spotter plane directed the tactical air strikes. F-4s and A-6s screamed in on the forest dropping either napalm or bombs. When we reached the base of the mountain, we had helicopter gunships on station should we need their firepower. I turned to Pete, "I don't know why we are going into those woods; there can't be anyone alive after that." Before Pete could reply, a column of Vietnamese women, old men and children came pouring out of the forest. I watched in disbelief. There must have been over one hundred stunned souls coming out of the smoldering woods. Some had bloody wounds, but the vast majority didn't have any visible wounds. The Captain gave an order and a platoon moved to secure the "civilians." The Vietnamese were put in a detention camp set up in the clearing at the base of the mountain.

Lieutenant Kim asked us to call in some helicopters that were bringing in another Korean Company and to evacuate the Vietnamese. After the first two CH-46s arrived, the reinforcing company took over the responsibility of guarding and evacuating the "civilians." Pete and I found the two Anglicomen, Rex and Budweiser, who had arrived on the first helicopter and briefed them on the situation. Then, we entered the smoky tree line with our company.

The HQ group followed the same path in that the Vietnamese had walked out on. Small fires were still smoldering, and the smoke stung my eyes as we walked deeper into the forest. 26th Company's three platoons were sweeping in front and to both sides as we met more Vietnamese walking out. Some were helping wounded countrymen. The Koreans held them until it looked like the stream of refugees had ceased and then sent them back, under guard, to the detention area.

We heard no gunfire as we continued our trek through the forest. It seemed that while the massive bombardment had not killed everyone, it had certainly destroyed their will to fight.

I paused as we entered a small clearing. Thirty yards ahead and to the left of the trail stood a large bombed-out stone Catholic Church. The roof was gone and the left rear corner had partially collapsed. A scarred but intact stone cross still stood at the top of the door-less entry way. Pete and I followed the Captain, Lieutenant Kim and a couple of Korean radio operators inside. The interior was one large room, empty of everything but rubble. The Captain went to the far corner of the room and sat down with his back against the wall. The Korean radio operators were talking to the platoons and relaying the reports to the Captain. The stone walls looked like they would provide excellent cover, and I helped Pete take the radio off. I leaned my rifle on the wall, dropped my helmet and flak jacket, and sat on the floor next to Pete on the opposite wall from the Captain.

As I rested, I reflected on where I was. I was in a house of worship. South Vietnam had a large Catholic population and apparently, some of them had lived in these woods. The missionaries that built this church had picked a beautiful spot. I thought of the people who must have worshiped in the church, now in ruins, and wondered if they thought it would ever come to this. Maybe some of the Vietnamese that came pouring out of the woods this morning had worshiped here. In spite of its current state, I still felt a sense of reverence for where I sat.

Every now and then, a couple of KMC would come in with more Vietnamese to be interrogated by Lieutenant Kim. When it was decided that they had no information, the prisoners were escorted back to the detention area.

I looked up as two KMC privates came in the door escorting an old, hunched over, skin and bones toothless woman to the Captain. He was talking with one of his platoons on the radio, and with a glance, he decided that this white haired old hag didn't have any information he needed and waved the two KMC privates to take her away. They each took one of the old woman's bony arms and started to escort her out. I stood up to stretch as they walked by, and one of the Korean escorts smiled at me and made a "cutting throat" motion. I am pretty sure it was a joke. The old woman saw the "cutting throat" motion and freaked, tore loose from the two KMC privates and ran to me. She fell to her knees, put her hands together as if praying, and pleaded with me for mercy. She saw the two KMC guards coming over to retrieve her, and she stopped praying and wrapped her arms around my legs and held on. I gave the two guards a disgusted look and tried to convince the howling old woman that no harm would come to her. But we had a language gap, and she continued to wail as the two privates tried to pull her off my legs.

All of the commotion caught the Captain's attention, and he stood up and started to walk over to us to see what the problem was. The desperate, tearful old woman decided that the Captain might be in more of a position to help her than I, and she released my legs and ran away from her guards to the Captain. Once again, she fell to her knees to plead for her life. It was a pathetic scene. The old woman was rapidly moving her pressed hands up and down, praying to the Captain. The Captain barked an order to the two guards now standing at attention behind the old woman. She screamed as they picked her up by her arms and pulled her outside. I followed them and stood in the doorway as I watched the three of them walking on the path leading back to the detention area. The old woman was still sobbing, but had stopped struggling with her guards and seemed resigned to her fate. After they disappeared into the woods, I stood at the doorway of the church and braced myself for a shot. I was relieved when I didn't hear one. I went back into the church and sat back down by my gear. Pete hadn't moved from the wall, and after I sat down by him, he said, "Crazy ol' woman." I took a deep breath and slowly nodded my head in agreement, "Yeah. Crazy ol' woman."

We slept in the church that night. I awoke at dawn and walked outside the church to answer nature's call. The Koreans were stirring and Moon was cooking breakfast. I went over to Moon and put in my breakfast order, "Yama sao K asakee, bop E D wa!" That was the bad phrase Sergeant Lee had taught me to say to Moon on my first day with 26th Company. Moon laughed, and I smiled at him as I patted him on the shoulder.

Around ten that morning, we heard some firing to the west. The Korean radio operators were getting the reports and Lieutenant Kim informed us that we had a medivac. Pete and I geared up and went with our four man security team to the medivac. *It was during medivacs that I missed Sergeant Lee the most. His command of the English language helped us understand what was going on.*

When we reached the wounded Korean private, we learned that he had been the victim of a sniper. The Koreans had killed the sniper and were deployed around the opening we were going to use as a LZ.

Pete and I checked out the wounded private to see how critical the wound was. He had a chest wound which was considered an "emergency medivac." Pete had the radio and called it in while I searched the Landing Zone for booby traps.

We sat on a log, lit cigarettes and waited. Fifteen minutes passed, and there was still no sign of the medivac helicopters.

As I flicked my second cigarette butt away, I looked over at the badly wounded Korean. A couple of his comrades were kneeling over him along with the Korean Corpsman, and they were trying to comfort their friend. One of the wounded Korean's friends glanced over at us and saw me looking. He stood and walked over to me. With tears in his eyes, he simply said, "Anglicoman, please."

I took a deep breath to control my emotions. I stood up, put my arm on his shoulder and told him, "Tee tee time."

"Soon." A few minutes later, we heard the familiar "wump-wump-wump" of helicopters. He was still alive when we put him on the helicopter.

After the medivac, we went back to the church. Two hours later Lieutenant Kim informed us that one of the other companies was heavily engaged with the enemy and that our company was to reinforce that company. We had to call in helicopters and be heli-lifted to the embattled company.

We had not cleared the forest yet, and it was suspected that a considerable enemy force remained nearby. The evacuation was not without risk. Because of its defensive advantage, it was decided that we should climb that mountain again and evacuate from there. We geared up and moved to the east out of the forest. Then we climbed that "number f.ckin' ten" mountain again.

For the first time, in addition to the CH-46s, they sent us an H-53. The H-53 was a very large helicopter with a large cargo capacity. It was better known by its nickname, "Jolly Green Giant."

The top of the mountain was not large enough or flat enough to land a helicopter. Pete and I searched for someplace we could call a LZ. The best place we found required that the helicopter land its back wheels on the top of the mountain and hover over the edge while we loaded. This time, dust was not as big a problem as were the small rocks. We had to turn our backs as the helicopters hovered to protect ourselves from the flying small rocks. They lowered their ramp, and the Koreans rushed in. With the help of "Jolly Green," we evacuated the mountain in only a few sorties. I was very impressed with the skill of the helicopter pilots, and we evacuated the position without incident

Pete, after we had built our bunker for the night. Just after Pete jumped down a nasty snake crawled out of the log.

The Church

Chapter 12
Just like in the movies

I cannot say with any certainty where we landed. *I wish that I had my maps and the Battalion log books to refer to now. Those two items would be invaluable helping me in this narrative.*

It was a clear area, and we landed without a problem. We deployed and waited for orders. Soon we were joined by two USMC M-48 tanks and two LVTs. A 106mm re-coilless rifle was mounted on top of one of the LVTs. *The 106mm recoilless rifle is a line-of-sight bazooka type of weapon that packs a nasty punch. The tanks each had a 90mm main gun and a heavy .50 caliber machine gun mounted on top for the tank commander.*

After the armored vehicles joined us, we started to sweep to the southwest to relieve 27th Company.

We had stopped in an open area when we saw the first elements of 27th Company passing though our company. Pete and I watched for the Anglicomen. Pretty soon, we saw them walking our way. Rex was wearing the radio and looked like a combat Marine in his KMC uniform, helmet and flak jacket. His M-16 was hanging over his shoulder by the rifle sling which was attached to the front sight mount and the butt of the weapon. Budweiser had a large Vietnamese straw sun hat on and was wearing cutoff Korean camouflage trousers and "Ho Chi Mien" sandals. The only thing that distinguished him from a beach bum and a Marine was that he still wore his flak jacket and was armed with his M-16.

They stopped and visited for a little bit. I complimented Budweiser on his uniform. He laughed.

The "Uniform of the Day" for Anglicomen in the field was pretty much whatever you felt like wearing that day, anything from KMC camouflage uniforms to USMC olive drab jungle uniforms to USMC jungle camouflage uniforms to Budweiser's non-uniform. His non-uniform was the most extreme I had seen. I always wore my Korean Camos while on operations. I am sure that it would have shocked a USMC officer if he had seen Budweiser. As long as we made the Koreans happy, they didn't care what we wore. In spite of the lack of "uniformity," we always did our job well.

27th Company returned to their C.P., and we dug in for the night. We did not build bunkers because the LVTs were not carrying sandbags; we only dug foxholes. We were also low on ammo as we had not been resupplied since the "Church operation." It was too late in the day to call in resupply, so we had to make do until morning.

Five hundred yards to the southwest was a large forest. That was the most likely place an attack would come from, so the tanks and LVTs were deployed facing the forest. Pete and I went to Lieutenant Kim with our map and marked the positions of all of the company's elements. Lieutenant Kim was concerned about the ammo situation and told us "Maybe Spooky tonight."

After a skimpy dinner of a c-ration can of pears and crackers, we lay down in our foxhole and went to sleep. We had only been asleep for a couple of hours when the night exploded into the largest battle I had been in.

Weapons ready, Pete and I crouched in our foxhole and tried to assess what was going on. Light and shadow danced by the swing of the descending flares, punctuated by bright flashes and striped with red and green tracers. This deadly light show was accompanied by music from hell. The tank to our right fired his main gun. I felt the concussion of the 90mm gun and was momentarily blinded by the flash. I felt someone jump into our foxhole. We turned to see Sergeant Lee. He shouted over the din that the Captain wanted a "Spooky."

Pete had already turned on our radio, and he called Past One Four. He advised Past that we had an "Emergency Request for Spooky." The battle raged on. I knew that ammo could be a problem, and it seemed that the outgoing was not as intense as it had been. The crash and flash of the tanks firing beehive rounds and their machine guns was reassuring. *Beehive rounds converted the tanks main gun into a giant shotgun that sprayed the area with little steel darts which were very deadly against personnel at close range. I think the tanks saved our ass that night.*

It is hard to give the battle an accurate description. Things were happening too fast. The mind would try to absorb one event when it would be torn away by another and another…

In twenty minutes, we established radio contact with Spooky, and Pete gave him our positions and the target area. Spooky dropped a flare, and before he had even fired, the enemy fire dropped significantly. On the next pass, Spooky opened up in front of the Korean's positions and the incoming stopped.

We had casualties from the battle, and we called in a medivac to take them out. With Spooky on station, the enemy chose not to fire on the helicopters, and the medivac was as uneventful as a night medivac can be.

We continued directing Spooky for an hour until he was relieved by a flare ship. Spooky had to return to base for ammo and fuel but would return if we needed him. The night had settled down, and Pete went to sleep and I stayed up to run the flare ship. The flares carried by the C-130 were in large, approximately three or four foot metal canisters. If the flare was dropped close, one could hear the metal canister make a low and slow, "woop, woop, woop" sound as it tumbled downward. Once we had a KMC casuality from one of those canisters falling on him. Now, only the drone of the flare ship, the popping of flares and the "woop woop woop" of the canisters disturbed the silence.

The flare ship dropped a flare on each pass, and I corrected his drop if needed. "Night Sky One Three, this is Scorcher Bravo, please drop the next flare 200 meters south of your last." If I didn't correct him, he assumed that he was dropping them where I wanted them and would continue dropping flares on each circle until I corrected him.

This day had started when I woke up at dawn in the church. We had a medivac, an emergency evacuation from the mountain and a long walk after we landed. Then, after we had about three hours sleep in our hole, the large midnight battle had interrupted our rest. I looked at my watch in the light of the last flare. It was a little after three in the morning. It had been a long day, and in spite of myself, I dozed off. I woke with a start and saw the flare ship was dropping the flares miles from us, pretty much doing no one any good. I thought, "O gigdy madda son?" Which translates roughly as: "Are you kidding me?" I didn't want to tell the flare ship I had gone to sleep and that he was miles away, and I couldn't come on the radio and tell him to drop his next flare two miles to the southeast. I called him, "Night Sky One Three, Scorcher Bravo, drop your next three hundred meters southeast." I slowly zigzagged him back to our area.

No one seemed to notice that the flare ship had been miles away. 26th Company, as well as the enemy, was exhausted, and I am pretty sure that the only people awake for miles around were in the flare ship, and, for most of the time, me.

The flare ship stayed on station until the eastern sky started to lighten. I turned the two knobs on the radio to "Scorcher One Four's" frequency and called Battalion. I recognized Red's voice and told him I was securing (turning off) the radio. I went to sleep the moment I closed my eyes. Pete woke me with a c-rat can of hot instant coffee at about 8:00. After I sat up and rubbed the sleep from my eyes, I sipped my coffee. "Good," I thought, "cream and sugar." Pete told me to drink up; we had resupply coming in half an hour. We had not taken any fire since Spooky came on station last night, but we told the chase helicopter that he was clear to fire into that forest to the southwest. We received our much needed resupply of ammo, food and water.

After the helicopters left, the Koreans were busy resupplying with ammo and making breakfast. We were hungry and the rice, kimchi and soup smelled good. Pete and

I walked over to where Mr. Chin was eating and sat down by him. Moon brought over our breakfast, and we sat and ate together.

After breakfast, Pete and I went over to Lieutenant Kim and asked what the plan was. We were going to assault the forest. We examined the wood line through the Lieutenant's binoculars. Between the three of us, we identified what we thought was a bunker in the tree line. At 0900, a USMC OV-10 spotter plane gave us a call. Pete popped a smoke grenade, and I gave the OV-10 the compass bearing and distance from the smoke to the target, the suspected bunker.

The company was deployed in a wide assault formation, and the two tanks and the LVTs were dispersed within the line. Since I had given all the necessary information to the spotter, I climbed onto one of the tanks and sat down behind the turret and waited for the air strike. The OV-10 fired two willy pete rockets on the suspected bunker, and the jets came in one at a time. The first F-4 Phantom dropped 250 pound snake-eyes and the second dropped napalm.

The combined infantry and armored assault started to move forward as the second jet came in. The tank I was riding on started forward with a jerk, and I almost fell off. I found a more stable position and held on as we rolled forward. The whole line was firing as we moved toward the tree line at a walk. A Korean .30 machine gunner to the left of the tank I was riding on fired long and sustained bursts at the tree line, laying down covering fire. With a rocking jerk, my tank stopped, and the turret rotated as they searched for a potential target. On my right, about fifty yards down the line, the LVT fired his re-coilless rifle. I was expecting the tank I was riding on to fire. I did not expect the blast of the 90mm gun to be as violent at it was. The tank rocked on its suspension at the recoil of the main gun. After he fired, I held on as we jerked forward to keep pace with the infantry. I looked around at the attack. It did look like something out of the movies. Being a part of that infantry/tank assault almost made up for my missing the amphibious landing.

We entered the woods without taking any casualties. The Koreans found quite a few dead enemy soldiers and blood trails. That night, after we had cleared the forest of any bad guys, Pete and I had supper with Lieutenant Kim. He told us that the "suspected bunker" had indeed been a bunker, and the air strike had destroyed a machine gun and its crew. We had done our part.

A couple of days later, Lieutenant Kim came to us and told us we had a medivac. We followed him through a crowd of KMC standing outside of a little shack. We followed Lieutenant Kim as he stepped inside the shack. On the dirt floor, a Korean Corpsman was assisting a young, suspected V.C. woman who was giving birth. After the Corpsman delivered the baby girl, he announced the birth to the KMC who were waiting outside. They all wanted to see the baby. We called in a routine medivac for mother and baby.

The operation ended on December 18, and after we went back to 26th Company C.P., Pete and I were relieved, and we went back to Battalion.

We were glad to be back. Pete and I had a couple of week's worth of mail and packages waiting for us. It was a week before Christmas and all the guys were getting Christmas goodies, and we all sampled each others edible gifts.

I had a lot of mail from Debbie. She continued to be the perfect fiancée. Mom was doing her part and asked Debbie and her family down for a dinner. Rex came in from 27th Company, and we quickly adjusted to Battalion life.

On Sunday, the 20th of December, I was on the afternoon radio watch. One of the Korean Lieutenants I knew came over to me. He asked if my name was "George." I told him that it was my first name, but no one called me by that name. He told me that, "George," then he spelled my last name, "was going to be awarded the "INHUN" the day after tomorrow." I told him that I was the guy.

We spent the next day shining our jungle boots and picking out our best Korean camouflage uniforms. One of the new guys asked me why I was getting a medal. I told him that I didn't deserve it any more than any of the other old guys did, and that it represented their actions as well as mine. I was just gonna get to wear it.

The next morning at 11:00, Sarge marched the six of us to our assigned position to the left front of the stage. *That was the only time I marched anywhere in Vietnam.* The Koreans had a large formation complete with a color guard and a small band. The Anglico Major, who looked like a postcard Marine, came out from Brigade. He was seated on the stage along with Captain Bodkin and half-a-dozen Korean officers. The Korean Colonel in command of 5th Battalion approached the mike and gave a small speech, of which I understood very little. He then motioned for me, and

I climbed the stairs, faced him, saluted and stood at attention. As the Colonel read the citation, one of the Korean Captains I knew translated for the benefit of the Americans present. The Colonel then handed me my citation and pinned the medal above the left pocket on my Korean uniform jacket. I would be lying if I tried to be modest and said I was not proud.

What I told the new guy earlier, when he asked about why I had received the medal, was true. Many of the other Anglicomen with the Koreans deserved that medal as much as I did, few received it. I feel very grateful and a little guilty for the honor.

After he had pinned on the medal, I saluted him, did a left face and marched off the stage to my spot in the Anglico formation. The Colonel dismissed us, and we watched a Korean USO show they had trucked in. After the show, we had a big lunch of rice, kimchi, soup and beer with the Korean officers, Korean USO show people and the Anglico major.

That evening, I asked Sarge to take a walk with me. As we walked along the beach, I told him I was not sure that I deserved the medal more than some of the other guys, and it bothered me. Sarge was quiet for a little bit and then he told me,

"Maybe not, but wear that medal with pride. You will find that in life many times you will feel that you are not appreciated. The Koreans have shown you their appreciation with that medal. Be grateful whenever anyone appreciates your efforts."

People have often asked me why the Koreans gave me a metal. I didn't do anything heroic like charge a machine gun or anything like that. The citation was dated 9 September, 1969 and reads:

"In recognition of and appreciation for his outstanding service to the cause of peace and freedom, I take great pleasure in awarding, in accordance with the powers delegated to me by the Constitution of the Republic of Korea, the: ORDER OF MILITARY MERIT , INHUN to Lance Corporal George Scott Leis, 2409915, United States Marine Corps.

"Participating as a member of Allied Forces fighting in Vietnam, he has devoted himself to safeguarding peace and freedom in Free Asia by displaying his superior ability.

"Furthermore, his close cooperation with and positive support to the Republic of Korea Forces, Vietnam have contributed to the achievement of their brilliant victory.

"His brilliant achievements, together with his personal devotion to the improvement of amicable and fraternal relations between our two countries, have earned our highest esteem and admiration, reflecting a great credit upon himself and the United States Marine Corps."

Then it was signed by the President of the Republic of Korea, "Park Jung Hee."

The Koreans gave me the medal because the Captain of 26th Company liked me, and he thought I did a good job for them. It was, by far, the best report card I ever took home.

On Christmas Day, we went to the MACV compound in Hoi An for a Christmas Dinner. We were on our best behavior.

INHUN

Sergeant James Baker

KMC formation for my INHUN

Living With Dragons

Receiving INHUN from the Colonel of 5th Battalion. The Korean mess hall is behind me. Our bunker/hooch is off-photo to the right of the parade ground. The South China Sea is in the background.

Anglico Major at front, Capt. Bodkin to his rear at my Inhun Ceremony

Just like in the Movies

Chapter 13
Bad Sea and Bad TV

On the third of January, we started a Battalion size operation. We sent one of the new guys, Vance Capehart, out to join Budweiser at 27th Company. Vance was a snuff dipper, and he always had a big dip of Copenhagen tucked under his lower lip. We changed his name from Capehart to "Copenhagen." Better than "Worm," I must add.

Captain Bodkin, Red, Rex, Pete and I went on the operation with Battalion Forward. Sarge stayed home at Battalion Rear. The duties of the Anglicomen on an operation at "Battalion Forward" were pretty much the same as when we didn't have an operation. We still had to maintain a twenty-four hour radio watch. The major difference was that someone shot at us every now and then, and the living conditions were much worse at "Forward."

The operation was a quiet one with little contact with the enemy. So on the 17th of January, Rex and I went back to Battalion Rear and Sarge came out to Battalion Forward.

Rex and I were overjoyed. We had the whole place to ourselves, and we didn't have to stand radio watch. The first day back, we just rested and slept a lot. By the third day, we were ready to go body surfing in the sea.

It was monsoon season and the sea was rough. As we stood at the water's edge, we marveled that we had never seen the waves so big. Perfect for body surfing!

We ran into the surf and swam out to catch a wave. My swimming skills had not improved since I went swimming with Pete and Sergeant Lee in the river, and I struggled against the violent sea. I caught a wave and rode it in as far as I could. I decided that I was not a good enough swimmer for this, and I tried to stand in the neck deep water to walk back to the beach. My legs were swept out from under me, and I was pushed further from the shore. Panic attacks a person whenever that person is in an unfamiliar situation that he/she deems dangerous. Panic hadn't attacked yet, but I saw it peeking at me over the next wave. I swam as hard as I could toward the shore, and when I couldn't swim any more, I stood up in chest deep water. Once again my legs were kicked out from beneath me by the undertow, and I was swept away from my goal. Panic saw an opening and struck. I swam like my life depended upon it and this time, when I stood up, I was in waist deep water. I was barely able to withstand the undertow as I started the struggle to reach dry land. As I was fighting forward, I looked to my right where I had last seen Rex. I was relieved to see him about twenty yards away fighting to reach the shore. We struggled to escape the sea that wanted our souls.

Exhausted, we reached the shore about the same time and fell face first onto the wet sand. We lay there for a few minutes, and then Rex stood up, walked over and sat down by me. I rolled over, sat up and wrapped my arms around my bent knees. Neither one of us said anything for a long time as we stared at the angry sea. I looked at him,

"You can't swim worth a damn."

He laughed, then asked me,

"Why didn't you save me?"

We both laughed. We helped each other up and walked back to our hooch.

I wrote to Debbie that night, and told her that Rex and I were just about "lost at sea." Later that evening, after we came back from the Korean mess hall, we made a tape together to send home to Debbie and her roommate at college. In reality, it was just a recorded B.S. session. *I wish I had that tape.*

The next day, we walked down to the sea. The waves didn't seem as big today as they were yesterday, but we had no desire to go "body surfing." As we sat on the beach, we could see fish jumping out of the water. Rex had an idea and turned to me,

"Let's go see the Korean Lieutenant and see if he will give us a Blooper!"

The M-79 grenade launcher was nicknamed "Blooper" because of the sound it made when fired. It resembled and operated like a single-shot sawed-off shotgun. It could lob a 40mm grenade about 400 yards. The grenade exploded on impact and had a kill radius of about five yards.

We went down to the TOC and entered the bunker. We walked over and sat in the comfortable chairs on either side of the Lieutenant who was in charge while everyone was on the operation. We made small talk for a little while and then Rex asked him,

"Lieutenant Som, you like fish?"

The Lieutenant replied that he did indeed like fish, all Koreans like fish!

Rex offered the deal.

"You give us one M-79 grenade launcher and one box of ammo, and we bring you fish!"

Lieutenant Som thought about it for a moment and then told us that we had a deal. He gave an order to one of the Korean privates. The private picked up a field telephone handset and made a call. As we chatted with Lieutenant Som, two KMC came into the bunker. One was carrying the Blooper and the other was carrying a case of ammo for it. We thanked Lieutenant Som, walked out of the TOC carrying our toys and headed toward the beach.

Rex and I spent all afternoon taking turns shooting at fish in the sea. When the stunned or dead fish drifted in, we would wade out and bag Lieutenant Som's dinner. We had a ball, and I am sure we were "over limit." The Lieutenant could have guests for dinner with his bag of fish. After we ran out of ammo, we took the fish and the "Blooper" back to the Lieutenant.

For the taxpayer that is shocked at the waste of tax dollars, we figured it up once. You were paying us twenty-two cents an hour. You got a deal.

On the 2nd of February, the operation ended, and everyone that was on the operation came in. We started keeping a twenty-four hour radio watch again. We had a lot of people to stand watch, so it wasn't bad.

The next day, the Anglico Major from Brigade came out. He told Pete and me that on Friday, the 6th of February, six Anglicomen were to testify at a "Board of Inquiry" in DaNang. The Koreans had been accused of atrocities on the Barrier Island Operation. Pete and I were to represent 5th Battalion. I asked the Major what a "Board of Inquiry" was like. He told me that we would be questioned by a board of high ranking officers about the Korean's conduct on that operation.

Pete and I spent the whole next day putting a spit shine on our beat-up jungle boots. When we were done with our boots, they looked like a mirror; well, maybe a cracked and scratched mirror. We found our best KMC uniform and put it to the side. We went to the Korean barber so that he could make us look military again.

Visiting the Korean barber more than once was a testament to my courage. The first time I had to get a haircut, I walked over to the Korean barber hooch, about fifty meters to the south of our hooch. It was reassuring that it looked something like a barber shop and was equipped with two barber chairs. The Korean barber couldn't speak a word of English, and I motioned that I would like a haircut. He turned the chair to me and I sat down. After my haircut, he tilted the barber chair back and lathered my face. I closed my eyes as he shaved my face with a folding hand razor. He shaved my neck, my forehead and my earlobes. I felt his cool hand on my forehead, and then I felt the cold steel sliding over my eyelids. I held very still and prayed that nothing happened to make this guy jump. It was over in seconds, and I was grateful that I didn't lose an eye. To this day, I won't close my eyes whenever I get a haircut. - That would explain my hairy eyelids.

Friday morning, Pete and I joined the other four Anglicomen that were going to DaNang at LZ Dusty. There was a helicopter waiting for us, and we flew to DaNang. The Major met us when we got off the helicopter and led us to a large office building. We were told to have a seat in a waiting room, and he explained that the board would call us in one at a time for questioning. After each of us was questioned, we would be dismissed and put in a separate room from those who were still waiting to be interrogated. *They did not want the first guy out telling the others what kind of questions to expect.*

I was the third man called in. I walked to the front of the room and faced the officers who were seated at long tables arranged in a "U." In the middle of the center table were two "full bird" Colonels flanked by Lieutenant Colonels and Majors. Other lesser grade officers sat at the two side tables. I snapped to attention and reported,

"Corporal Leis, reporting as ordered sir."

The Colonel on the right gave me, "At ease, Corporal."

On the wall behind me was a large map of Barrier Island. They asked me if I had been on the operation in question. I replied that I was with 5th Battalion's Forward Command Post. They provided me with a pointing stick and asked me to indicate on the map where we were and what we were doing. I pointed to the location on the map where 5th Battalion Forward was. Then I tapped where the three companies of 5th Battalion were and what they were doing. They asked how long I had served with the Korean Marines. I told them fifteen months. It was quiet for a little bit. Then one of the Colonels asked me, "Corporal, did you see, or hear of the Korean Marines doing," he paused, "anything unusual?" I honestly answered, "No Sir." He thanked me and then dismissed me. I exited out a side door to join the two Anglicomen that had already testified.

After all six of us had been questioned, we waited outside for our Major. After about fifteen minutes, he came out and told us that the board was impressed with our military bearing and professionalism, and he was proud of us. Then he took us to a real American mess hall, and we ate lunch.

I never heard anything more about the inquiry.

I don't know what happened to the prisoners that day on Barrier Island. I didn't ask Rex, and he didn't volunteer any information. Maybe the Korean Captain paroled them all and sent them on their merry way. There was a phrase used extensively in Vietnam. That phrase was: "Yeah, maybe. But I kinda fuc.in' doubt it."

After lunch, we asked the Major if we could go to the American PX as we seldom had the opportunity. He said that we could, and we went to the PX to spend some of our money. My little tape recorder was on its last leg, so I bought a more expensive one.

That evening, in our hooch, I was messing around with my new tape recorder. Sarge and Pete were sitting with their backs to me watching Bonanza on Pete's TV. Rex was at the table writing a letter. My new tape recorder had a neat feature, a wireless microphone that had an on/off switch to remotely start the tape recorder from about fifteen feet away. After reading the manual, I found a little screw on the back of the microphone. I turned the screw to adjust the frequency so the mike could communicate with the recorder. As I was turning the screw, I noticed that when I turned it to a certain spot, the wireless microphone interfered with the TV. If I left it on that frequency, the television would lose its picture completely. When I shut the mike off, the picture would clear up. Cool!

I shut the mike off, and the picture cleared up. Sarge quit trying to adjust the television's rabbit ears and sat back down to watch Little Joe duke it out with a bad guy. I called Rex over. He knew that I was up to something, and he pulled up a folding chair, and we sat behind the TV audience. I whispered to Rex,

"Watch."

I held the mike in front of him and turned it on. Sarge immediately started cussing and stood to adjust the picture again. Just as he reached the TV, I turned the mike off and Sarge returned to his seat. Rex smiled. I waited a minute and then flicked the switch to "on" again. As he started to get up to fix the problem, Sarge told Pete, "Your TV is a piece of sh.t, Plummer!" Pete told him, "Just sit down and hold your horses, it'll clear up!" They sat and watched snow for a full minute waiting for the picture to clear up. I was quite certain that it wouldn't. Only the annoying buzz of the television disturbed the silence. Finally, mumbling to himself, Peter got up to adjust the TV, and I shut my mike off just before he touched a knob. Pete threw his arms up in frustration, and Rex and I could no longer hide our giggles. Pete and Sarge turned to see why we were laughing and they saw the mike in my hand. I am afraid that Rex and I were the only ones who appreciated the humor.

Rex and I laughed and giggled a long time as we talked about how Sarge and Pete had gotten so angry. Then Rex remembered that the Koreans had a large TV mounted above the radios in the TOC. We smiled at each other and plotted our electronic attack on the Koreans.

The mike had a two foot wire antenna attached to it that I had to hide. I put on my "poncho liner jacket" that the Vietnamese laundry had made out of a poncho liner. I draped the wire around my neck under the jacket and put the mike in my trousers pocket with my thumb over the on/off switch. We stood, and I flicked the switch to make sure we were still on the right frequency. Sarge and Pete started cussing at us again. I turned it off, and Rex and I walked down to the TOC.

We walked into the TOC, said hi to Red who was on radio watch, and stood at the entry way into the Korean radio room. We looked to our right and saw that the comfortable chairs were all occupied with Korean officers watching the last half hour of Bonanza. Rex and I made sure that nothing war-like was going on that we would interfere with.

It was a quiet night, and I turned on the wireless mike. Bonanza was replaced by snow and a loud buzz. No one moved for thirty seconds. Then one of the Korean officers barked an order to a Korean radio technician.

The tech ran across the room to the TV. I turned off the mike just as he touched the large television and Hoss was fighting half a dozen bad guys in a saloon. As the tech turned to go back to his seat, I flicked the switch. The tech hurried back to the TV, and I made it right again.

Rex and I didn't want the tech to get Kodabaca or be punished in any way. We approached the technician who was standing to the side of the TV to make sure that it maintained its picture. As we walked up to the tech, I turned the mike on and the Korean started to work on the television. I asked him, "You want me fix television?" He anxiously looked at me, "You can fix?" He was clearly concerned that the officers were getting a little frustrated. I said, "Yes." Then, with my free hand, I snapped my fingers in front of the screen and the picture returned.

This time, Little Joe and Hoss were fighting each other. The tech looked at the picture and at the hand that I had used to snap my fingers. He said, "Accident." I said in an incredulous voice, "Accident?" and snapped my fingers in front of the screen and scrambled the picture.

We played that game for a little while, and then I asked the tech, "Why all time TV number 10?" The Korean radio technician explained that the TV was being interfered with by all of the radios in the TOC. He demonstrated using an imaginary handset that was being keyed. I told him that I understood, and Rex and I proceeded to have a conversation on imaginary handsets. Every time one of us would key our phantom handsets, the TV went on the blink.

The Koreans watched their TV and our hands in stunned silence. Rex and I decided that we had had our fun. I turned the switch to "off," removed my hand from my pocket, and we turned to leave. As we walked out the door, we paused to look back. Half a dozen Koreans were gathered around the television, snapping their fingers and keying imaginary handsets.

We walked back to our hooch. Our electronic attack had been successful.

Another one of the features of my new tape recorder was an attachment that fit on the back of a telephone handset. I tried it out one night while on radio watch, and I recorded everything that seemed interesting. I don't have that tape anymore; I probably re-recorded some music on it or something. So many things mean so little until you lose them forever.

Rex and I entered our hooch just in time for "Star Trek." Sarge and Pete reluctantly allowed us to join them for our favorite show. I pulled up a chair by Pete, and we watched Captain Kirk duke it out with an alien.

Rex and me (Rex photo)

My poncho liner jacket.

Chapter 14
Smoke Anyone?

When I first walked into Battalion with Corporal Willis to meet Jim Marshal, the place was a dump. The ceiling leaked and soaked poor Randy when his poncho collapsed. Now, we had painted all the walls white, the only color of paint we could get our hands on. We had a brand new, large sleeping quarters with Air Force bunk beds. Someone figured out how we could build a shower using a strong wooden frame with a 55 gallon barrel mounted on top. We asked the Koreans for the wood and an old diesel barrel. Sarge sent home a request for a stock tank heater. We rigged a rope to a shower head, which was attached to the base of the barrel to turn it on and off. Since we had to climb ten feet up a ladder to fill the barrel, we always tried to conserve water. It was great when we had it all fixed up. Someone would climb up the ladder to the top of the barrel and light the tank heater. Thirty minutes later, three or four guys could have a short hot shower before we had to refill the barrel. For the first two weeks, we all smelled like diesel fuel; kept the mogies at bay though.

Sarge got a hold of a couple of bottles of whiskey which he used to trade with some U.S. Navy Seabees for some concrete. One morning, a U.S. Navy six-by truck equipped with a crane pulled up to our hooch. Sarge gave them his two bottles of Jim Beam, and the Seabees unloaded an approximate five foot square rubber bag of concrete. We had voted to make a patio / basketball court with a four foot tall concrete wall surrounding it. The total area would be about 20x20 feet.

Mixing the concrete was a chore. We didn't have a mixer, and we used a 55 gallon barrel to mix it in. We had to tote the water in 5 gallon fuel cans and mix everything by hand. Sarge decided that we needed gravel. I had never seen gravel in Vietnam. Pete suggested that we drive down to the old Buddhist temple that was already half destroyed and crush the stone walls to use as gravel. We drove past the ruins every time we went anywhere. Sarge gave the OK and I threw a sledge hammer in the back of Banard as Pete slid in behind the wheel. Pete took the beach instead of the road, and we raced through the waves like we were twenty-year-olds.

We almost missed the temple because we had never seen it from the beach. Pete picked a lightly wooded area, and we drove through the trees toward the ruins. He pulled up to one of the walls and turned Banard off. I had seen the temple a hundred times, but I had never explored it.

It was a quiet and pleasant morning with only the surf and a few birds disturbing the silence. I walked around the building and carefully studied it. I had the same sense of reverence that I had when Pete and I were in the bombed out Catholic Church.

Pete had retrieved the sledge hammer from the back of Banard and was looking for a place to start destroying a wall. I stopped him,

"Pete, wait a little bit. Let's just take the walls that have already fallen, it will be easier."

He paused as he was getting ready to swing at one of the standing side walls. He let the head of the sledge drop to his side. "Ok, I guess we can do that."

There was a truck load of fallen walls, and we worked all morning breaking them into pieces we could carry. We were home with our "gravel" by lunch time.

We were pretty good at laying the cement floor, and we all found a place to write our names before the cement dried. *While looking at an old photo of "Guns," the pig, on the patio, I saw my name in the concrete. I remembered the day fondly.*

We finished our patio and with the exception of the four foot walls, it looked like a professional job,. We had built a frame of plywood to pour our walls, and the weight buckled the plywood between the supports and it turned out like modern art. One of the guys got a hoop and a basketball from home, and we had many heated two vs. two and one vs. one games of basketball on our patio.

On February 16th, I broke a promise to Debbie and myself and volunteered to go with Pete out to 27th Company C.P. to relieve Budweiser and the new guy, Capehart, for a couple of weeks. There were no operations coming up for a while, and Budweiser and the FANG deserved to go back to Battalion for awhile.

As we pulled off the main road to go on "27th Company Trail," we could see the top of the new seventy foot tower they had received. The drive was still considered dangerous as occasionally vehicles would be sniped at. The trip went without incident.

The tower was the only visible improvement. Unlike

the changes made at Battalion, 27th Company Anglicoman bunker was just like it was the first day I came out here with Corporal Willis to give Lewis his mail.

Most days were quiet, and Pete and I played cards a lot. The cards were so worn and sticky we had to powder them with talcum power so we could play. We were playing poker with paper matchsticks that represented money, and I had a run of bad luck and was down hundreds of dollars. Pete was tiring of the game and suggested that we cut the cards for "double or nothing." I agreed and lost. Pete said, "Ok, let's cut for double or nothing again." My run of bad luck was still alive and before I knew it, I was, according to the figures that Pete was keeping, down just a little more than one million dollars. I said,

"Alright, let's cut again."

Pete lay down on his cot and said, "Nope, I'm done."

I stopped shuffling the cards, "What do you mean, 'I'm done'"?

He leaned up on his elbow to look at me over the table, "Yep, I'm done." He looked at his piece of paper, "You owe me one million, three hundred and sixty dollars." Then he lay back down on his cot.

I was quiet for a little bit. I asked him,

"Where the heck am I gonna find a million dollars? Where the heck am I going to find three hundred and sixty dollars?" Then I informed him, "Debbie is really gonna be mad."

He assured me that we could work out a payment plan at a reasonable interest rate. He thought a monthly payment of $10,000 at 3% interest was fair.

He made me beg a long time before he agreed to cut the cards again, but only after I had signed a piece of paper he drew up stating:

"Date:
    I, G. Scott Leis, aka "Worm," owe Peter Plummer $1,000,360.°°.
Signature:
Rank:"

I signed the stinking piece of paper, and he checked my signature to make sure that the document was in order. He was satisfied with the signed IOU, and we cut the cards again for "double or nothing." I was relieved that I finally won the cut. I tore up the IOU and never played poker with Peter again.

One afternoon, I was sitting on a sandbag wall outside my bunker with one of the KMC privates. He was cleaning his rifle and smoking a Korean cigarette.

Korean "tombays," the Korean word for "cigarettes," were awful. The tobacco tasted bad, and unless they were deeply and often inhaled, they would go out. Often the Koreans asked us for American cigarettes. We couldn't supply the whole Korean company with our cigarettes, so we seldom gave them away. The Koreans had the unusual practice of clinching their cigarettes between their teeth as they smoked; probably because they had to continually puff on

Smoke Anyone?

them to keep them lit.

Although we were sitting only half a foot apart, we were not paying any attention to each other. He was concentrating on cleaning his rifle, and I was in the middle of a science experiment with some C-4. *C-4 is the high explosive clay-like substance used in claymore mines and as a general explosive.*

I had taken one of my Marlboros out of its pack and had carefully twisted three-fours of the tobacco out on a sheet of writing paper. I was careful not to lose any of the tobacco because later in the building phase, I had to repack the cigarette. I picked up my little block of C-4 and broke off a BB sized piece. I rolled it between my thumb and forefinger into a small ball that would fit inside the void the removal of the tobacco had created. I carefully dropped the ball into the cigarette casing on the remaining tobacco. I thought about it and decided to put a couple more little balls into the cigarette. After I was satisfied that the charge was sufficient, I picked up a twig off the ground and carefully tamped the loose tobacco back into the cigarette. After I had tamped the tobacco in as well as I could, I evaluated the finished product. It was a little too heavy and the tobacco would probably fall out in time. I doubted that I could pass it off as a real cigarette. But I wanted to see if it would ignite the C-4. I carefully lit the cigarette and had started to place it on the ground to watch the experiment, when I remembered the Korean sitting next to me on the sandbag, clinching his cigarette between his teeth.

The devil is alive and well.

I smiled at the KMC as I tapped his shoulder. He

looked at me as I offered the lit cigarette and asked him, "Tombay?"

He had been so engrossed in his task of cleaning his rifle that he had not even noticed what I was doing while I constructed my booby-trap cigarette. My sandbag mate was shocked that I would offer him an American cigarette without his asking. He removed his cigarette from between his teeth and threw it on the ground, where it promptly went out. He took my offered lit cigarette and said, "Com hom som D da," which means "Thank you very much."

I smiled as I nodded at him and sat back as he bit down on the cigarette and resumed concentrating on swabbing the barrel of his M-16. I scooted a few more inches away on the sandbag.

I had played with C-4 enough to know that it would not explode. I had even used it to rapidly boil water for instant coffee. When touched with flame, it reacted much like loose gunpowder but with more intensity.

In the interest of science, I looked at my watch and marked the time to judge how long my fuse was. I didn't stare at him as that might cause suspicion. Out of the corner of my eye, I watched the progress of the red tip of the cigarette, and when the smoking end reached a critical point, I faced him and looked at my watch. At one minute and five seconds, the C-4 ignited. Eyes wide, the Korean private dropped his rifle and started slapping his face with both hands trying to knock away the flame throwing tombay clinched between his teeth. I thought it was just about the funniest thing I had ever seen. He finally slapped the cigarette from his face and, although he was not hurt, he called me every nasty Korean word I knew and a few new ones I had never heard before. Still giggling, I offered him a generous gift of five C-4 free Marlboros as an apology and assured him, "Tombays, oopsa (*no*) booby trap." He cautiously accepted them but was still pretty huffy as he picked up his rifle and cleaning gear and left. I continued to giggle as I sat there and recalled him slapping his face. *Sweet Ma would have said, "That wasn't very nice," but no one was hurt and I got a good laugh and that always feels good. I still giggle when I think about it.*

One night during the second week Pete and I were at 27th Company C.P., we took some fire from one of the wood lines in the distance. No one was hurt but the next morning the Captain asked us to call in an air strike.

Pete and I made a deal with each other. He would carry the radio up the tower and after the air strike, I would carry it down. I let him get about halfway up and then I followed. We ran our air strike and prepared to go back down the ladder.

Pete helped me put the radio on, and he started the climb down. I waited until he was about half way down and then I started my descent. I loved the view from the tower but hated the going up and coming back down part. I slowly and carefully made my way to the ground. When I finally felt solid earth beneath my feet, I took a short sigh of relief and turned around to see Pete standing right in front of me.

He was tossing a smoke grenade up and catching it, and for some reason, he had a scowl on his face. I studied his face and the smoke grenade he was playing catch with. I reached over my shoulder to feel the two smokes that we had hung by their spoons on the radio backpack. There was only one. I started to laugh and he gave me a good rap on the head with the smoke. He told me that he was just over halfway down when the smoke grenade hit him on the head and almost knocked him out. In spite of the fact that I was rubbing my head from his sharp whack, I was still laughing as I apologized. He turned on his heel and walked back to our bunker. Chuckling, I followed him. We were both rubbing our heads.

On the seventh of March, Sarge drove Budweiser and his counterpart back out to 27th Company C.P., and Pete and I went back with him to Battalion.

When we arrived at Battalion, Sarge introduced us to a couple of U.S. Marines that had joined us at 5th Battalion. They were not part of Anglico, and I do not remember why they were attached to the Koreans. I also do not recall the name of one of the Marines, but I became friends with the other. He was the biggest Marine I had ever seen. He was as large a man as Mr. Chin and because of his large size, he was nicknamed "Jolly Green Giant," or just "Jolly." He was as gentle as he was big, and he liked to laugh, all good qualities.

Pete and I joined Rex, Vance and Red, and we all shared the radio watch. Red and I had our last face-to-face chess game and on the 17th, Captain Bodkin, Pete and I drove Red to Brigade to begin his journey back to the United States. Unlike Pete and me, Red had not extended his tour in Vietnam and had only signed up for a two-year enlistment. He was going to get an "early out" from the Corps when he arrived back in the U.S. It was an emotional farewell as we said goodbye to Red. Pete and I drove back to Battalion in silence. Pete's "short-timer" calendar was down to twenty-two days before he rotated. I was down to fifty days.

Rex with Korean USO girl at party with the Korean officers.

Trail going into 27th Company C.P.

Running Air strike from the tower.

Smoke Anyone?

**Guns asleep on our patio.
Note names in cement.**

Relaxing in front of Mortar pit

Capt. Bodkin, Red, Pete

Smoke Anyone?

With Korean Captain and my captured flag and SKS rifle

Chapter 15
Ambush on the Beach

A couple of days after Red left, Rex, Pete, Sarge and I drove to DaNang. We were going to spend a night at an American RnR center, go to the PX and visit a "steam and cream," a Vietnamese massage parlor. I never have been a fan of cities, and I would not have gone at all except I wanted to order a set of Noritake china for Debbie at the PX.

Sarge drove, Pete called "shotgun" and Rex and I rode in the back of Banard. Sarge knew where he was going, and we pulled into the RnR center without incident. We ate good food, drank beer, and in a real theater, watched a movie about a German female spy in WWI. They gave us racks, and we slept in the next morning. We had a nice breakfast of pancakes, eggs and bacon, and then we went to the PX. I ordered one of the more expensive sets of Noritake china and arranged to have it delivered to Debbie's parent's home. Then, in readiness for my rotation, and because I didn't want all my money stolen in Okinawa, I sent home most of my money.

Sarge went to the mess hall and begged for some hamburger and buns to take back for a barbeque we had planned for the next day. The mess Sergeant gave us four or five pounds of frozen hamburger and a couple of dozen buns. He also gave us a jar of pickles, half a dozen onions, a can of ketchup and a can of mustard. We loaded our box of food in the back of Banard and went to the massage parlor. I didn't really want to go in so, I volunteered to guard our hamburger. I waited in the front seat for them to come out. It was early afternoon before we started our return drive to

Battalion.

As we were driving back, we came upon an accident on the road. We stopped as we drove past an overturned jeep. A U.S. Navy Corpsman was tending to an injured American, but there were two badly mangled, dead U.S. Marines that hadn't been covered up yet. Auto accidents can be just as ugly as booby traps. *The accident is still very vivid in my mind as are most of my serious medivacs. I do not like gross descriptions of the casualties of war. To write this narrative, I must look into that "dark place" in the back of my mind, but I intentionally try to avoid using graphic descriptions.* We had our radio, and we asked if they needed us to call in a medivac. Someone had already called it in, so we drove on.

Because I had the midnight to six radio watch that night, I took a nap when we got home.

It was a quiet night and I was rereading Bruce Catton's book "A Stillness At Appomattox," when I smelled the unmistakable odor of marijuana. I turned in my chair and saw one of the Korean Lieutenants I knew standing behind me taking a drag on a joint. I asked him,

"Lieutenant, what is that you smoke?"

He looked surprised that I would ask and held up the Vietnamese rolled marijuana cigarette and explained,

"Oh this, this is Vietnam cigarette. I have no Korean cigarettes, I have no American cigarettes, so," with a shrug, "I smoke Vietnam cigarette."

I nodded my head,

"Is it a good cigarette?"

He smiled,

"Oh yes! It is a very good cigarette!"

I told him,

"I will tell your Colonel you smoke Vietnam cigarettes."

"Oh no! No you must not tell the Colonel I smoke Vietnam cigarette." He paused as if deep in thought, "No, my Colonel does not like Vietnam cigarettes!"

I assured him that I would not tell his Colonel and resumed reading my book.

At six, I called Past One Four and told them I was shutting down for five minutes while I woke my relief. He acknowledged, and I signed off on the log book.

I went into our sleeping quarters and shook Red awake and told him that it was time for him to go on watch. Then I went to sleep to rest up for our beach barbeque that afternoon.

We had a great going away party, and Sarge presented Pete and me with "short-timer-sticks". Short-timer-sticks were elaborate Vietnamese made canes, and it was a tradition to give them to people that were about to rotate back to the United States.

It was late afternoon before we walked back up to our hooch, and we waited for our shower water to get warm to wash the salt and sand off of us. A Korean ran to our door and yelled, "Anglico, medivacs!"

We had not heard any gunfire, but we grabbed a radio and followed the Korean as he ran out the door and toward the beach. To the north, we could see two U.S. Marines supporting a third man between them. They were slowly limping toward us on the beach. We ran to them. All three had multiple gunshot wounds, but the man being carried by the other two had a bloody leg wound and was in a lot of pain. All had lost a considerable amount of blood and the Korean Corpsmen were treating their wounds. The least seriously wounded Marine asked us to call his unit. We changed to the frequency of his unit and gave him the handset.

They were part of the U.S. Marine tank Company next to the LVT Company south of Brigade. They had gone to Da Nang in their jeep pulling their trailer so they could get supplies and had decided to take the beach home instead of the road. They were ambushed on the way home, and the jeep and trailer were shot up pretty bad. There were four of them and a couple of them had been wounded in the initial burst of gunfire. All the tires were shot and had gone flat, and the jeep got stuck in the sand. One of the unwounded, a Corpsman, jumped out to unhook the trailer which was loaded with supplies. As he started to get back in the jeep, another burst of gunfire from the wood line had hit all four men. The driver had floored the accelerator, and the Corpsman fell out of the jeep and was left behind. They decided that they were too badly wounded to try and return for him, and since they were still being shot at, they made a run for it. Their jeep gave up the ghost, and they abandoned it a thousand meters north of 5th Battalion C.P. They limped into our compound.

The guy that borrowed our radio told us that his unit was sending a tank and an LVT down to search for the Corpsman who was left behind. After the Korean Corpsman gave him a shot of morphine, the Marine with the raw hamburger leg had stopped crying out in pain, and we waited for the helicopters.

A few minutes after the helicopters left, the tank and LVT pulled up to us on the beach. They stopped and asked about their wounded. We told them about the wounds and that they were probably in the hospital by now. The tank commander asked if two of us could go along in case they needed a medivac or air support. I had no intention of volunteering, but when Rex jumped up and said he would go, I again broke my promise of "not volunteering."

Rex and I ran up to our hooch and put on our flak jackets and helmets and grabbed our M-16s. We ran back down to the waiting tank and LVT, climbed aboard the LVT and Sarge handed me the radio.

The sun was setting, and it was going to be dark soon. The LVT followed the tank north along the beach. The LVT was a headquarter's vehicle and, unlike all the other LVTs I had ridden on, it did not have the sandbag protection or the .30 machine gun. I felt very exposed.

The tank was faster than we were, and he was outpacing us. It rounded a curve in the beach and disappeared behind the trees. When we rounded the curve, I saw the tank a hundred and fifty yards ahead in the twilight as it was driving past the disabled jeep. I looked at the jeep as we drove by it. Its hood was up, it had four flat tires and it was full of bullet holes.

It was getting darker all the time, and I thought of the Corpsman we were looking for. It must be terrible to be wounded and alone on the beach in the dark. I tapped Rex on the arm and yelled at him over the noise of the racing LVT,

"Rex buddy, if I get shot, don't let me fall off of this thing!"

He looked at me and yelled back, "Don't worry, I won't leave you behind, don't leave me behind." I promised that I wouldn't, and I relaxed a little bit.

It was dark when we pulled up to the tank and the trailer. The tide was rising and the surf had erased the tracks around the empty trailer. Keeping an eye on the wood line, Rex and I jumped off the LVT onto the soft sand. Using flashlights and the search light mounted on the tank, we joined the LVT crew and the tank's crew as they searched the beach for their comrade. We never found him, and after an hour of searching, we mounted up and headed home. The Koreans found the American Corpsman washed up on the beach a couple of days later, and we called in a "routine" medivac for him.

Is it any wonder that some people came home and cannot put that war to sleep? I do not find fault with anyone involved with that incident. If the other three wounded

Marines had tried to go back for the Corpsman, all four would have washed up on the beach a few days later. But I am grateful that I do not have the nightmare of the decision to leave him behind haunting me. Sleep well brother, you did what you had to do.

The Koreans were all very helpful in the "ambushed jeep" incident. They sent patrols following behind the tank and LVT, although they were on foot and were quickly outdistanced by the tracked vehicles. It was one of the KMC patrols that found the tanker's dead Corpsman two days later.

After serving with the KOREAN MARINE CORPS for eighteen months, I had come to a few conclusions concerning their attitude toward America and Americans.

I never met a Korean that did not love America. They loved America second only to their own country. I was told by Sarge that as a Corporal in the U.S.M.C., I made almost as much money as a Korean Captain did. Either I was vastly overpaid or he was vastly underpaid. Since I liked my standard of living, I had determined that he was vastly underpaid.

We were rich beyond their imagination. They were not jealous. They desired to work their way to become "same-same America!" The Koreans saw the rewards of a free democratic society, and they felt it vindicated their form of government. They were *and are* great allies, and I was *and am* proud of them. They knew all the great American historic heroes and, more importantly, American pop culture heroes.

Whenever an English speaking Korean new guy would join either at Battalion or at the Company level, one of his early goals, if possible, was to "practice his English on the Anglicoman." Most of the time the first thing they would say to us would be,

"Anglicoman, you know "John Wayne?"

Smiling I answered that I had heard of "John Wayne."

Nodding his head the Korean would reply,

"Yes, John Wayne is very famous American movie star."

My part: "Yes he is."

"Anglicoman, you know Elvis Prezley?"

After I told him I knew who Elvis Presley was, the KMC would inform me that,

"Elvis Prezley is very famous American rock and roll singer."

"Yes, he is a very famous American rock and roll singer," I replied with a smile.

I had that exact conversation dozens of times. I always enjoyed visiting with them, and always did my part and told them what they wanted to hear. Well, almost always.

Once, in the TOC, during an interview by an English speaking KMC who was accompanied by a half dozen of his buddies, we had the following encounter:

It was a quiet afternoon on radio watch, and I paused in my letter writing to think of something else to write to Debbie. I noticed the group of Koreans. They were gathered around each other and were discussing what they would say to open their dialogue with me. They settled on "Elvis Prezley" and approached me. The English speaking Korean asked,

"Anglicoman?"

I stood and faced him. The common acknowledgement was,

"Maua."

"Anglicoman, you know Elvis Prezley?"

I wrinkled and massaged my forehead and thought long and hard as I tried to recall the name,

"No," slowly shaking my head, "Never heard of him."

Shocked, he paused. He was certain that he had mispronounced one of his American idols and one of his best spoken English names. It could not be possible that an American had never heard of "Elvis Prezley." He slowly repeated the name,

"ELLVIS PREZZLEY."

"Nope, never heard of him. Korean man?"

"No! Joe con A! Very famous American rock and roll singer!" Then he started singing, "Ruv me tender, ruv me true."

"No, never heard it." I asked, "Korean song?"

He shook his head,

"O gidgy madda son?" which roughly translates as "Are you kidding me?"

The Korean looked at me in shocked silence for ten seconds. The rest of the delegation then demanded a translation. The Korean turned to them and translated our conversation. The whole group erupted in disbelieving gestures and questions. They discussed what they should do next and it was decided. The Korean faced me, and in his very best English,

"Anglicoman, you know "John Wayne?"

"Who?"

"JOHN WAYNE! JOHN WAYNE! VERY FAMOUS AMERICAN MOVIE STAR!"

I thought for a moment and then started to shake my head "no." He threw up his hands in frustration, turned to his buddies and started swearing. They discussed what to do next, and it was decided that they were out of ideas. The "Talk to the Anglicoman" delegation walked away shaking their heads. I sat back down at my radio and, with a new story to tell Debbie, resumed my letter.

Never underestimate the power of laughter. Yes, I have gotten many laughs from friends and family when telling this story. But the Korean that I had the discussion with probably gets his share of laughs from his buddies about how he met the stupidest American ever. "The American that never even heard of Elvis Prezley or John Wayne" story is probably among his favorite Vietnam stories.

In the year and a half I had been with the Koreans, I had learned to communicate with almost any Korean through a combination of English, Korean, a spattering of Vietnamese, a few French words and hand gestures. Sometimes it took longer than other times, depending upon how much English the Korean I was talking to knew. Like a language never used, I have forgotten much of what I learned. I apologize for my bad Korean.

Rex, Pete, Red and I routinely walked the perimeter of 5th Battalion. We would stop and visit with the different positions that the KMC manned. We always enjoyed our visits. If one of the positions was testing its machine gun, we would ask to fire their weapon. As long as the Colonel wasn't around, they obliged us.

The Korean motor pool was on the far southeast end of the compound. Parked there were a couple dozen six-by-six wheel drive trucks, half a dozen ¾ ton vehicles like Banard, and the same number of "mules." Mules are a small, U.S. made four wheel drive vehicle. It had one seat for the driver on the left front. The driver's seat was level with the rest of the four foot wide and six or seven foot long flatbed.

It was much like a large goofy looking go-cart that could haul supplies. I had even seen 106mm recoilless rifles mounted on them.

One day I walked over to the motor pool by myself to have a closer look at the mules. As I was looking at one, the KMC Sergeant in charge of the motor pool came over and started visiting with me. Again, I never met a Korean that was not immediately friendly with us. He spoke very little English but seemed happy to have met me.

Every Korean knew that if they were hurt, their ticket out started with us. Or it may have been because of their love for America that they treated us so nice. Maybe they are just a polite people. For whatever reason, we were given every courtesy. I pray that I was worthy of their friendship.

While I was visiting with the KMC motor pool Sergeant, I climbed behind the wheel of one of the mules. He asked, "You like?" I replied that I did like his mule. He asked me, making a steering motion, "You drive?" I told him, "Yes, I would like to drive!" He gave his OK and I raced up and down the beach and around the compound all afternoon. It was great fun, and when I returned the mule to the motor pool, I told the Sergeant, "Com hom som D da," which translates "thank you very much." He bowed his head, and as I walked back to our hooch, I thought about when I could find an opportunity to play with the mule again.

The next afternoon, I repeated my experience of the first day, but on the third day, the motor pool Sergeant met me at the mule, shook his hand back and forth and said, "No Anglicoman. My Colonel say no give Anglicoman mule!" I told him that I understood, and I asked him if he got in trouble. From what I could understand, he only got yelled at a little bit. I apologized for any trouble I got him in, shook his hand and went back to our hooch.

The Colonel was quite justified in not wanting the Anglicoman turning his compound into a go-cart track. I overstepped myself, and I consider my action disrespectful.

The motor pool Sergeant and I became friends, and I went to visit him many times, and a few times he even came to our hooch to visit with me and the other Anglicomen. It seemed that all the Koreans were fast learners, and his English improved at a greater rate than my Korean.

I had lost my chess partners when Captain Bodkin and Red left. I taught a couple of the new guys, Ed and Vance, how to play RISK. I warned them that I was a "Field Marshal" in RISK. I proved I was worthy of the rank by winning more than my share.

The FANGS were all good guys, and I enjoyed their company. But I missed all of my old buds. It felt like forever ago when I said goodbye to my original RISK opponents, Don and Gettle. It seemed like with the new guys, I was trying to recapture a moment in my past. It just wasn't the same.

At times, I think I still try to "recapture" some of those moments. A good friend has always said: "Live in the present, the past is gone, and the future isn't here yet; you only have the present." A very wise and true statement. I do love this moment in my life, but the times I spent in the Corps were special moments. It is often said that: "The Service will make him grow up!" It failed miserably in my case. I don't think I have grown up yet. But while it may not have made me "grow up," it did teach me, among other things, how to recognize a "friend." It is not hard to understand why many servicemen have given their lives so that their friends could live. I felt that way with my "friends" because I knew they would do the same for me. I try to choose my friends based on that criterion.

Pete was down to twelve days before he rotated to the United States, I was down to forty days.

Beach Party

Living With Dragons

Tank on the beach

Rex

Chapter 16
Goodbye Vietnam

Many times helicopter gunships would go "feet wet" going from or coming back to DaNang. Whenever an aircraft entered the Korean's area of operations, they had to check in with Past One Four, Brigade to get clearance. If there were any artillery missions going on in our zone of operations, Past would inform the helicopters of the path and the altitude the shells would reach. The aircraft would take measures to avoid that altitude and area to prevent it from being hit by friendly artillery fire. Unless there was a reason to fly through our area, it was just simpler to fly "feet wet" over the sea.

I always admired the job that the Brigade Anglicomen did on the radio. Brigade is where John went after he left 26th Company a year ago. John had rotated home when his original tour was up, and because he had only signed up for two years, he was a civilian by now. While on radio watch at Battalion, I only got involved in the conversation if part of 5th Battalion was involved. The radio operators at "Past One Four" were always busy. It seemed everyone had their own style on the radio, and "radio protocol" was lightly adhered to. For example, in my two weeks of radio school, we were taught that when we finished our part in the conversation the correct thing to say was "over." If we were not expecting an answer and we were finished talking, the correct term was "out." That was the first rule of "radio protocol" to fall to the wayside.

One of the Brigade radio operators that I admired was a Corporal I had met when I went in to visit John. His name was Phil, and he had a very unique radio style. He was always calm and collected on the radio, and the last thing he always said before he unkeyed the microphone was, "Roger Roger."

"Roger Roger" never bothered me. He was an excellent operator, and whenever I had to call Brigade, whether it was for an "emergency request for 'Spooky' or just a 'radio check,' I was glad when he was on duty. "Roger Roger" did bother somebody up the totem pole, and Phil was informed that he used "Roger" too often. The next time he was on duty, he changed "Roger Roger" to "oakie dokie." A couple of days later, the person that was offended by "Roger Roger" told Phil that he could go back to his own style.

Helicopter pilots did not like taking unspent ordnance back to base. Practice makes perfect. Many times while I was on radio watch at Battalion, the helicopters checked in with me to see if the Koreans had a potential target. I asked them to "wait one,," and I went to the Korean Officer in charge in the TOC and asked him if he had a target. I then informed the helicopter if there was a target or not. Many times the only target the helicopter could find were fish in the sea.

Shortly after dawn one morning, we were awakened by the roar of many trucks going by our hooch and heading north up the beach. We ran out to see what was going on. The whole compound seemed to be on the move toward where the trucks had stopped, about one hundred yards from the perimeter. We ran over and stopped a Korean and asked him what was going on. He said something that none of us recognized and took off. We followed to see what was important enough to draw hundreds of the Koreans to the beach. As we approached, we could see that the Koreans were using long ropes and chains to tie onto something in the sea. Dozens of KMC were in the water, and twenty 6X6 trucks were forming two tow lines of ten trucks each. Hundreds of Koreans were getting set to have a tug of war with a whale that was killed by helicopter fire and had washed up about one hundred feet offshore.

It was a marvel of engineering to behold. It looked like a scene out of "Gulliver's Travels." After three solid hours, twenty trucks and hundreds of KMC, in and out of the water, they won their prize and the whale was beached. I asked one of the officers why they wanted a whale. I guess that was a stupid question, because he looked at me in disbelief. "Whale, joe ossa!" (Whale, good!)"

I had helped them in their quest on one of the rope lines, and I was hungry. After I had them take my photo sitting on the whale, I went to our hooch for a late breakfast. As I was leaving, they started butchering their whale.

I went out a few hours later to check on their progress. The whale was almost gone. The Koreans had taken every piece that could be used for anything and were carrying large pieces of blubber to their quarters. A strong fishy smell overtook the compound. That evening, two KMC came to our hooch and knocked on our screen door. We opened it, and they offered us a piece of blubber the size of a large pillow. The smell almost overwhelmed us, and we recoiled from the doorway as we tried to explain we really didn't want any. I believe we even used the word "Joe D ca!" which means "GO AWAY!" They were shocked we would refuse such a great gift.

After a couple of days, the blubber must have started to rot because the smell only intensified. Over the next two weeks, we either got used to it or it dissipated.

To anyone that is shocked at the helicopter's killing of the whale, read the label for war: "WARNING: TWO OF THE <u>GUARANTEED</u> SIDE EFFECTS OF WAR ARE SENSELESS KILLING OF ANIMALS AND WANTON DESTRUCTION OF NATURE." And the label goes on, and on.

Make sure the benefit is worth the side effects before you swallow that pill. Sometimes it is, sometimes it's not. Either way, you can always expect the side effects.

Two days later, just when the smell of the dead whale had reached its apex, Sarge and I drove Pete into Brigade to start his journey back to Maine.

We had all stayed up late the night before, drinking and talking about all the things Pete and I had seen and done together. We concentrated on the stories that made us laugh.

Pete had been my counterpart at company level more than anyone else. We probably knew each other better than anyone else in the world would ever know us. Pete was truly like a brother. He always had my back. We both stayed strong as we wished each other good luck and shook hands goodbye. *And, I never saw Pete again.*

I was down to twenty-eight days before I would follow Pete home to the United States.

A couple of days later, "Jolly," the big Marine that

had joined us about a month ago, came to me. He was excited because he had made contact with one of his old high school buddies. His friend was an enlisted man in the United States Air Force and was stationed at an Air Force base in DaNang. Jolly wanted me to go with him to visit his pal. Although I was leery of going to the big city, Jolly was insistent that I go along. If there was anyone I felt safe, with it was Jolly. His massive size would probably ward off any trouble we might run into. I agreed to accompany him to Da Nang.

We called a Huey that was on its way back to DaNang and asked him to give us a ride. The Huey landed on the beach, and Jolly and I hopped in. I never went anywhere unless I was armed with my M-16 and fully dressed as if I was going on an operation. The only thing Jolly and I left behind was the radio. We landed in Da Nang and found the Air Force base.

I was stunned by the base. Some Marines stationed in the United States didn't have quarters as nice as the Air Force guys had here. I felt like I was at a "costume party," and Jolly and I were the only ones in costumes. We went as two U.S. Marines dressed as Korean Marines on an operation; the only thing missing was the radio and the dirt. Everyone else was dressed as Air Force guys who were stationed in the United States. They seemed as shocked at our "choice of costume" as we were of their base.

We found Jolly's friend's hut and knocked on the door. Jolly's bud opened the door, and they greeted each other. Jolly introduced me to his high school pal, Will. Will then introduced us both to the other three guys in the nicely furnished bedroom. As I recall, there were about six beds to a building. Jolly and I were going to sleep on the two extra beds that night.

All the Air Force guys were friendly, and they asked a lot of questions about what we did and what it was like doing what we did. I have never thought that "bragging" was a good quality in a person, and I tried to keep it low tone and concentrated on the funny stories. I did however, answer any questions they had as truthfully as I could. The truth is enough.

My Dad was a great guy, but he liked to stretch the truth sometimes. I always told him, "Dad, when you exaggerate the truth, you diminish the truth." I have tried to follow that principle in this narrative.

We visited with Will and his roommates until dinner time when we joined them in their mess hall. It was more than a mess hall. A cafeteria would be a more accurate description. We ate very well that night. After supper, we went to their on-base club. The Air Force base club was better that most clubs I had seen in the U.S.A. Jolly and I joined Will and a large number of Air Force guys at a large table. A Vietnamese rock band was playing in the background as Will asked what we would like to drink. My mixed drink of choice was a "Seven-seven," but after a little thought, and maybe a little macho, I asked for my whiskey straight. Jolly had the same, and in a flash, we each had four or five shots of whiskey in front of us. Try as I might, and I tried too hard, I never had less than four shots of whiskey in front of me. Airmen from other tables saw Jolly and my Korean costumes and gathered around the table to ask us questions and to buy us drinks.

We were half soused when a siren interrupted the band and everyone, with the exception of Jolly and I, lay on the floor. Some of the prone people were telling us to get down because Da Nang was under rocket attack. Da Nang is a big place. I tilted my head and listened for explosions. I couldn't hear any, and I asked Jolly if he heard anything. He said he couldn't, so we shrugged our shoulders and tried to catch up on our drinks. I joked to Jolly that it looked like 26th Company may have to go "rocket hunting again." Some of the airmen had overheard my comment about "rocket hunting," and after the "all clear" was sounded, they wanted to know about that operation.

By midnight, we were completely soused, and we staggered back to Will's hooch and went to sleep.

The next morning, we had a nice breakfast, and then we hitchhiked to the helicopters and went home. I thanked Jolly and I told him to thank Will and his friends again for being such gracious hosts.

A few days after Jolly and I came home from Da Nang, I developed a heat rash on my back. It was miserable, and it seemed that nothing I put on it relieved the constant pain. I guess that it was one of those things that just had to run its course.

A week later, we received a new Marine Corps Lieutenant pilot on F.O. duty. I cannot remember his name, and I only knew him for a week or two.

A few days after he arrived, the Koreans came to our hooch and told us we had a medivac about 1000 meters northwest of the compound. My heat rash was just about gone, and for some reason, I volunteered to go out to it. The new F.O. Lieutenant said he was also going . I geared up with all of my equipment, and Rex held the radio as I put my arms through the straps. The Lieutenant put on his helmet and flak jacket. His only weapon was his .45 caliber pistol.

Following our four-man security team, we went through a gate in the wire toward the medivac.

We were about five hundred meters outside the wire in a lightly wooded but densely bushy area when we started taking fire. The Lieutenant and I sought cover behind a small embankment and lay down by each other. I peeked over the top of the embankment to see what was going on, and the Lieutenant grabbed my shoulder and told me to get down. I explained that we only had four Koreans with us, and we might have to defend ourselves. The sporadic firing was still going on, and the Lieutenant turned to me and told me,

"Leis, give me the radio!"

I had never given up my radio in a combat situation to anyone in the almost nineteen months I had been in Vietnam, and I wasn't about to start now. I answered him,

"No sir, I will not give you my radio. If you want me to call in something, I will call it in, but I will not give you my radio."

He accepted that, and after a little bit he told me,

"Ok, give me your rifle."

I couldn't imagine giving up my rifle when people

were shooting at me, and I replied, "No sir, I am not giving you my rifle either."

The guy or guys that were shooting at us disappeared as suddenly as they had appeared, and we continued our trek to the medivac. The medivac went without incident as did the return trip to 5th Battalion's compound. That was my last medivac, and the last time someone shot at me.

The Lieutenant went into his sleeping quarters, and I walked into our main hooch. All of the other Battalion Anglicomen were in the room and asked me how it went. I explained what had happened and proceeded to tell them of the Lieutenant's silly requests that I give him my radio and rifle. As I was telling them the story, I noticed that the expressions on their faces changed in a way I did not expect. They seemed to be looking past me, and I turned to see the Lieutenant standing in the doorway behind me. He turned on his heel and returned to his quarters.

While I do not regret my decision not to give the officer my radio or rifle, I do regret that I did not use more discretion in relating the story to my friends. I should have apologized to the Lieutenant for belittling him to my companions. I didn't then. I do now.

The day before I was ready to begin my journey home to the United States, I took a walk around the compound. I went to the TOC and said my farewells to all of the Korean officers and men I had worked with. I made one more trip to the Korean barber (I kept my eyes open), and stopped by the motor pool to tell the Korean Sergeant goodbye. Then I went down and sat on the beach by myself for a long time and tried to accept that after tomorrow, I would never see this place again. The Anglicomen had often discussed that, if there was not a war going on, this area would make a beautiful beach resort. I packed light and only packed one of my KMC uniforms to take home with me. *I left much behind that I wish I had brought home.* I went to sleep listening to the waves of the South China Sea for the final time.

The next morning, Sarge drove me past the bombed out Buddhist temple for the last time. It looked the same as it did the first day I came out here. Sarge dropped me off at Brigade, and we shook hands and said goodbye. While at Brigade, I met Joe Medina, the guy that had his strobe light shot at by a helicopter. He had orders to report to the same place I was going. We checked out with Brigade. The Major gave us plaques with a "Sub Unit One, 1st ANGLICO" shield with our names underneath, and someone drove us down to the helipad. We got on a helicopter and started our trip home. I was going home on leave for a week, and then to my new duty station, MABS-32, MAG-32, MARINE CORPS AIR STATION, BEAUFORT, SOUTH CAROLINA. Joe and I promised to look each other up when we got there.

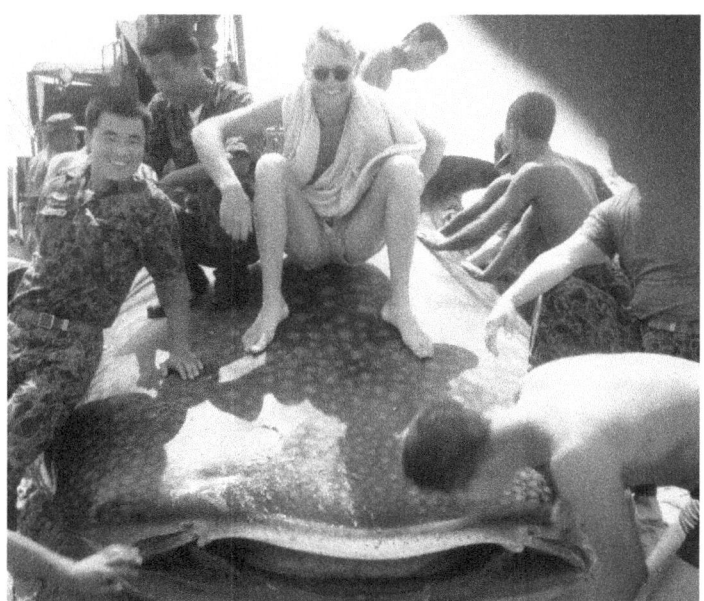

The Whale

Sunrise outside of 5th Battalion's Anglico hooch/bunker

Goodbye Vietnam

Chapter 17
BEAUFORT

I left Vietnam to finish my last twenty two months in the Marines at MAG 32 Communications, MARINE CORPS AIR STATION, Beaufort, South Carolina. Air wing! Air wing was known to be much more lax than Infantry. I was happy with my new assignment.

Joe Medina joined me a few days later. As we were the only people that had the same type of experience in Vietnam, we were inseparable. Debbie and I were married in July 1970, and she came to South Carolina with me. Joe married a girl from his home in Brooklyn. Joe and his new wife moved into a trailer in the same small trailer park where Debbie and I were living outside of the base.

I got along well at my communications shop. The shop was way out in the country to the side of the end of one of the runways. We watched the Marine pilots learning how to operate the HARRIER, a jet that is capable of vertical takeoffs and landings. I probably lost a little more of my hearing.

Comm. Chief, Gunnery Sergeant Nickols, liked to hear my stories about my service with the Koreans, and he liked to laugh, so we got along great. I had a serious problem with the second in command of the radio section, Sergeant PromotedBecauseHeReenlisted; hereafter to be referred to as Sergeant PBHR *pronounced "PEEBAR."* Sergeant Peebar had been a rear-echelon guy that served at some airbase in Vietnam. Because I got shot at and he didn't, I had twice as many ribbons as he did. He didn't like me, and I didn't care for him. I hated the fact that he had authority over me and despised taking orders from him to clean Prick 25s. *When I was with the Koreans, no one gave me orders. I hung out with the officers of the Company and was treated as an equal. When they wanted something, they said please. It was hard for me to adjust to taking orders from people I didn't respect.* So when Gunny asked for a volunteer to take care of the five or six generators we had, I jumped at the opportunity to get away from Sergeant Peebar.

The Generator Section was a one man section. I told Gunny Nickols that I needed the wire section's little storage building, which was located about seventy five yards from the rest of the shop where my generators were parked. Much to the Wire Section's Staff Sergeant's disgust, Gunny made him move his stuff out. Gunny gave me a desk and chair. I had electricity, so I had coffee, a radio and a fan. As a joke, I stenciled a sign over the door leading into my hut:

MAG-32 COMM. GENERATOR SECTION
CORPORAL G. S. LEIS, NCOIC
(NCOIC =Non-commissioned officer in charge)

I went to a school to learn how to operate and maintain various models of generators. I learned how to start them, put fuel in them and change the oil. Anything more serious than that, I noted in the generator's record book. I would enter why it was not working, and that it had been reported to the next higher level of maintenance. I was lucky if half of my generators were working at any given time. But I always did my routine maintenance work and diligently kept my record books accurate. I heard rumblings that the

Radio Section's Chief, Staff Sergeant Harris, Sergeant Peebar and the Wire Section's Chief were complaining to Gunny that Leis was just getting out of duty. Staff Sergeant Harris wanted me back as a radio operator, Sergeant Peebar just didn't like me, and the Wire Chief wanted his storage shed back. Gunny stuck up for me, and for the moment, I was safe.

One day, we had a surprise shop inspection from a dozen officers from up the chain of command. All the other sections in the shop, Radio, Wire, and Technicians, failed the inspection. My one man Generator section received an excellent. Ha, I had volunteered for this job just to get away from Sgt. Peebar and the drudgery of the Radio Section. From that time on, my job as NCOIC Generator Section was safe.

Because of my "excellent" on the surprise inspection, and because I had graduated second in an AN-TSC 15 radio van school in Camp Lejeune, North Carolina, Gunny put me up for "Meritorious Sergeant."

I was honored to be nominated for Meritorious Sergeant, but it meant I had to do a lot of studying. Debbie and I could certainly use the extra money that a promotion would bring. I reported to a building with half a dozen other hopeful Corporals. We were to go, one at a time, before a panel of a dozen officers who would grill the candidate on their MOS, Marine rules and regulations, different weapons and who knew what else. There were a number of different radios the Marine Corps used at that time, and they all had thick manuals. I studied as well as I could, but I was nervous when it was my turn to be interviewed.

The room and setup was much like the "War Crimes Board of Inquiry" I went to in DaNang, except the uniforms were dress instead of fatigues; and there was no map of BARRIER ISLAND behind me. I reported to the officers.

The Major at the center front gave me at-ease. He asked me what my MOS was. I replied that I was a 2531, field radio operator. "OK," I thought, "Here come the radio tests." He had my record book on the table in front of him and asked me about my service with the Korean Marine Corps in Vietnam. From that point on, my interview became a "Korean story session." I knew that subject well, and I had them laughing in no time. For fifteen minutes or so, I answered their questions about my experiences with the Koreans, and we were all laughing and having a good time. I thought, "Again, humor is serving me well. This is gonna be a piece of cake." Then, a Lieutenant asked me if I intended to make the Marine Corps a career. Without hesitation, and being an honest person by nature, I answered, "No Sir." It became very quiet. After an uncomfortable silence, the Major asked me how they could justify promoting me to Sergeant above a career-minded Corporal. Trying to recover, I explained that if they promoted me, I would teach the career-minded Marine how to be a good Sergeant. They dismissed me. I never heard who got the promotion, but it wasn't me.

Gunny could not believe that I had blown it. A few months later, he put me in for the base "NCO of the Month." He told me that if they asked me if I was going to make the Corps a career, tell them that "I was considering it." I didn't make that one either.

We were informed that there was going to be a

"Junk on the Bunk" inspection, the one where everything the Corps had issued us had to be all arranged by the book on a bed. The one I hated. Much to my relief, because many of my state-side uniforms were still stored in Okinawa, I didn't have to stand that inspection.

We were on a big radio exercise in support of a big exercise with the rest of the Air Wing. We were operating the big radio van that I had gone to school for at Camp Lejeune. Commercial electricity was providing the power, so they didn't need my generators, and I had to take my turn operating the radio. On the third day of the exercise, after I had been relieved of the morning radio watch, we had a big honkin' South Carolina thunderstorm. The radio van was out by my generators, and with a mighty crash, lighting knocked out the commercial power. We went off the air. It is not acceptable for a modern army to loose communications, even in an exercise.

It was raining like mad, but I felt this was my opportunity to prove my worth as MAG 32 COMM GENERATOR SECTION NCOIC and told Gunny I would get us back on the air in no time. I ran outside and jumped in a jeep and drove out to one of my working generators. I hooked it up and pulled it over to the radio van. By now, I was soaked and the thunder and roaring of the rain was deafening. I grounded my generator, hooked the necessary power cords to the radio van and started the generator engine. I was on my fourth button I had to push to get power to the radio when lightning struck the antenna on the radio.

The next thing I remember, I was flat on my back with the rain pouring on my face. I heard someone calling my name, and I turned my face toward the voice. It was my friend, Marc Bullock, the radio operator, yelling at me through the open door of the radio van. I was about fifteen feet away from my generator. I heard someone else yelling my name and turned my face toward the shop. Joe, Gunny and a dozen others were running toward me in the rain. "Oh no," I thought, "They think I'm hurt. I gotta get up and show them I am OK." I tried to get up but instead just flopped over on my face in the mud. I continued to try and stand but just flopped back and forth like a beached fish. Joe reached me first and helped me sit up. After a few minutes, I was able to stand, and soon I was none the worse for wear. *But, I have a good excuse for being a little weird!*

Just before Christmas, 1970, Dad had a heart attack. Gunny gave me emergency leave, and Debbie and I flew home. Dad was still in the hospital when we arrived. He was a cantankerous patient, probably because he hadn't had a cigarette for a number of days. *He never smoked again, and he claimed that the heart attack saved his life. He was probably right.* Debbie and I stayed through Christmas. Dad was home when we flew back to South Carolina.

Debbie got a job at a bank in Beaufort, and with the extra money, we were able to rent a small two bedroom house in Beaufort. Debbie's parents were very insistent that Debbie finish her college education, so she enrolled in some classes at the local community college. Joe Medina's wife had gone back to Brooklyn, and Joe often stayed with us in the spare bedroom.

One Saturday night, Debbie and I were almost ready to go the Navy Club when there was a knock at the door. It was Joe. Gasping for breath, wine bottle in hand and more than a little drunk, he came in and told us about his night. He was out drinking in some bar in town and got into a big fight with some civilians. He escaped by swinging a pool stick to keep his adversaries at bay, and then ran to our home. I told Joe that Debbie and I were going out for the evening to the Navy Club. Joe thought that was a great idea, and he was ready to go. I forcibly told Joe that he was too drunk to accompany us, and he was not invited. I crushed him. He lowered his head, said he was sorry for bothering us, and walked out the door. I shut the door behind him, sat down on the couch and bowed my head. I looked up at Debbie with a mist in my eyes. She told me to go get him. I ran out the door and started to get in my car to catch Joe, when he called my name. He was sitting against a large tree in our front yard. I walked over and sat down by him. He offered me the bottle of wine. We didn't go to the club that night.

I suppose that because I had more ribbons than most, Gunny was always assigning me to special type of duties. I had to, *or should I say,"was honored to,"* be part of the honor guard for a visit by the Assistant Commandant of the Marine Corps. We were standing a pre-visit inspection to make sure we were all squared away when my hearing, or lack of, almost got me in trouble. It was a full winter greens dress uniform inspection. The inspecting party consisted of our Captain, our First Sergeant, followed by a couple of Lieutenants. The Captain moved down the line and about every third or fourth Marine, he would do a right face to inspect and question the Marine. He did a right face in front of me. He looked my uniform over, and then looked me in the eye and asked,

"Would you like to button that button Corporal?"

I thought he asked if I was missing a button, and I was

sure I wasn't so I replied,

"No Sir!"

He had a look of shock. Out of the corner of my eye, I could see that the rest of the inspecting party was equally stunned. The Captain looked at me,

"Well Corporal, I would like to button your button, the First Sergeant would like to button your button, and," looking down the line, "everyone else would like to button your button. Why don't you want to button your button?"

I heard it right this time. I answered that I would like to button my button and proceeded to do it. He smiled, said "Thank you," did a left face and went to the next Marine. Good Grief.

The First Sergeant didn't move on. He stood facing me and almost hissed,

"When the hell were you in China, Corporal?"

Confused, I answered,

"I was never in China, First Sergeant."

"Then why the hell are you wearing the CHINA SERVICE RIBBON?"

I replied that I wasn't.

He tapped my Korean award, THE INHUN "What do you call that Corporal?"

I explained that ribbon was a Korean Award. He was somewhat skeptical until I told him about my service with the KMC.

I told Gunny about it later, and he told me to wear the medal inside of my jacket next time for proof. The experience did serve me well, however. My original INHUN ribbon was getting a little soiled, and it was almost impossible to get a replacement. I went to the PX and checked out the CHINA SERVICE RIBBON. Sure enough, it was a perfect match. I bought a couple of new ribbons.

I was also assigned to a color guard on the July 4th celebration for the civilian authorities in Beaufort. I was the rifleman next to the National Colors. We marched to our given spot in the open parking lot and stood at attention while the different town officials, in the shade of a covered stage, gave speeches. An open parking lot, at two in the afternoon, on July 4th in Beaufort, S.C., can be a hot place. We stood at attention for what seemed like forever and sweat was tickling my nose. I tried to keep from locking my knees. I noticed out of the corner of my eye that the Marine holding the American flag was kind of swaying. Sure enough, a few seconds later, he fell flat on his face. I reached out with my arm and grabbed the flag before it fell. The dignitaries must have taken that as a sign that they had spoken enough, and they brought the ceremony to a conclusion. We revived the flag guy, and other than a bump on his forehead and a scratched nose, he was OK.

We had to re-qualify with the rifle. The range was at MARINE CORPS RECRUIT DEPOT, PARIS ISLAND, which was just a short drive away. We met that Monday morning in front of the armory where we picked up our M-14 rifles. From there, we all boarded a Marine Corps bus and drove over to Paris Island. I had mentioned that Air Wing was pretty lax, and we looked it. Many of the guys on the bus were mechanics, and their utilities were stained with oil and had battery acid holes. Most boots hadn't seen shoe polish for a long time and were more white than black. We were a pretty salty lookin' bunch. We had heard that the Paris Island Drill Instructors would give their platoons about face if they saw us coming. No attempt was made to march us, and rather than, "Forward March," the order came out, "Come on herd." It was said that if one of the recruit platoons saw us, their Drill Instructors would tell them that, "Those guys are reservists."

They herded us into a big building with folding chairs facing a stage. We took a chair, and a Gunny, with a Smokey Bear hat, jumped up on the stage. In a loud commanding voice, the likes which I hadn't heard since boot camp, he introduced himself and told us that he was our Marksmanship Instructor. Then he addressed us,

"In the Marines, we have the OLD CORPS, we have the NEW CORPS and then we have that other f.ckin' bunch, and that's you people."

We cheered.

He told us the rules on the range. When we were at the 500 meter line, we were not to shoot the trash cans on the 300 meter and 200 meter lines. We were not to shoot at a recruit that was trying to escape. After some more rules, we were herded out to the range to start our four days of practice. In spite of the rules, every now and then, when we were on the 500 meter line, someone would shoot the trash cans on the 300 and 200 meter line. On Friday, we shot to qualify. I re-qualified.

A little more than three months before my enlistment was up, I was called into the Gunny's office. He told me that I had received orders to transfer to some Infantry unit in Camp Lejeune, North Carolina. I protested that those were stupid orders. I only had three months left, Debbie had a job, was in school and it was just ridiculous that I have to go to North Carolina. He tried to calm me down and said that he agreed. My only option to get out of these orders was to "Request Mast." I had heard of "Requesting Mast." It was a means for a Marine to try and right a wrong. I never dreamed I would use it. It was one of those things we had all heard about but had never seen it in practice. Oh well. I told Gunny that I wanted to "Request Mast." Gunny explained that I would have to go up the chain of command until someone fixed it, or eventually I would reach President Nixon. I was hoping it didn't go that far. The first on the Chain of Command was Gunny. He couldn't fix it, so I had to go see the Lieutenant. He couldn't fix my bad orders, so I continued up the Chain of Command through a Captain, a Major and then the Base Commander. Everyone that I pleaded my case to was very sympathetic and supported my cause.

Not so much the Base Commander. Colonel Scaryashell started yelling at me as soon as I reported to him at his desk. He told me that I could be sent to the brig for refusing my orders. I tried to plead my case, but he never stopped his tirade against me. He looked at my record book and said he did not understand why I would want to screw up such a good record. I replied that I didn't think I was screwing up my record. That only brought forth a new burst of profanity and threats. Then, in the midst of this asschewing, Colonel Scaryashell's First Sergeant came in and whispered in the Colonel's ear and showed him a piece of paper. The Colonel looked up at the First Sergeant, who gave a slight nod of his head. The First Sergeant left, and the Colonel's name changed from Scaryashell to Letsbealittlecivil. He looked up at me and gave me at-ease. So far, I had been at attention during the whole thing. I went to parade rest. In a very calm voice, he informed me that he could not do anything about my orders. I calmly told him that I understood, but I hereby request mast with the General. He took a deep breath and told me that was my right. With that, he dismissed me. I snapped to attention, did a smart about-face and walked out of his office.

I drove back to the shop and went into Gunny's office to tell him about my experience with the base commander. He told me that he had already heard that the piece of paper was from a Colorado Congressman asking about my case. Debbie had told her parents about my orders, and they knew the Congressman. It is said that there are only two things the Corps fears, Mothers and Congress. Gunny said that from now on my papers would show "Congressional Interest." He also told me that my next stop was standing tall in front of a Major General in charge of the 2nd MARINE AIR WING at Camp Lejeune, N.C. O gidgy matta son! If Colonel Scaryashell was this bad, how bad could a Major General be? What if this doesn't work? The next guy in line after the General was the Commandant of the Marine Corps, then the Secretary of Navy, then, I guess, ol' Tricky Dicky. Sheesh.

The only time the General could see me was the next Sunday morning. My First Sergeant and Captain offered to take me there. We left on a rainy Saturday morning for the day-long drive to Camp Lejeune. The NFL playoff games were on, and they had to miss the games on TV. We listened to them on the Captain's car radio. We stopped at a fast food place, and the Captain got sick. We had to stop every now and then so he could get out in the rain and throw up in the ditch. I felt terrible about this being my fault.

We arrived in Camp Lejeune, and they put us up for the night. The next morning my First Sergeant and Captain picked me up, and we drove to the General's HQ building. Because it was a Sunday morning, the large building and the many offices were vacant. They dropped me off in the General's Sergeant Major's office, and they went in to see the General. I felt sick. I dreaded getting chewed out by a Major General. The Sergeant Major came in the door, and I jumped to attention. In a very kind voice, he told me "as you were" and asked if I would like a cup of coffee while I waited to see the General. I gratefully accepted. After about forty five minutes of sweating it out, the General, my Captain and First Sergeant walked in the door. I jumped up and stood at attention. The General was a post card Marine. He was six four, all muscle and had a very commanding presence. The Captain introduced me to the General, who extended his hand. He shook my hand, put his other hand on my shoulder and said, "You can go home now son." I think I mumbled a question about, "Is it really over?" He assured me that it was. I thanked him, and he turned to my Captain and said, "I don't know why this had to go so far. I wish all my problems were this easy to fix."

I am forever grateful for the kindness given to me by my First Sergeant and Captain. They had no obligation and nothing to gain from that weekend but to help me out of a jam. Their conversation with the General saved me from "standing tall" in front of him. They put themselves on the line for me. They were "leaders" of Marines.

My experience with "Requesting Mast" was a moral boost for the rest of the guys in the shop. It proved that the system could work.

A few weeks later, we were having a party/barbeque at our shop. We were playing volleyball when Gunny called me over. He had three of his Gunny buddies with him for the party, and he asked me to tell them about getting struck by lightning. I told them the story and they got a good laugh. Then Gunny told them I also went to see the General. One of them asked me how I liked seeing the General. I told them that I enjoyed the lightning more.

When I had three months left in the Marines, I was eligible to attend a "Project Transition" course. This was a program designed to prepare departing Marines for a job in the "real world." I knew a guy that went to work for a radio station in Beaufort because he wanted to go into that field. There was a list of places we could go. I decided to go to a two week course for the United States Postal Service's clerk/carrier test. At the end of the two weeks, we took the test, and I scored an 87.3. Because I was a veteran, I got a five point bonus. I sent the score to the post office in Ft. Collins, Colo. Ft. Collins was the home of Colorado State University, the college Debbie was going to before we got married, and she wanted to finish her education.

Two weeks before my discharge, I received a letter from the post office in Ft. Collins granting me an interview for a job on March 7, 1972. I wrote back and explained that I would be discharged on the 6th, so I couldn't make it home by the 7th. I could make and would appreciate an interview on the 9th of March or later.

A week and a half before I got out, our entire shop, with the exception of me, shipped off to the Marine Corps base in Cuba for an exercise. On March 1st, 1972, I made Sergeant. The Captain who read my citation told me it was probably too late to help me much financially, but maybe it was a bit of prestige. I was grateful.

Before being released, I had to take another physical. Once again, with the exception of the hearing test, I passed with flying colors. The two Navy corpsmen could not believe how bad my hearing was. They asked me if I wanted to file for a disability. They seemed surprised when I told them "no."

On March 6th, 1972, 1,460 days after the yellow footprints, I was discharged. Debbie and I packed up and drove home to Colorado.

Beaufort

EPILOGUE

On the 9th of March, I went into the Post Office in Ft. Collins, Colorado and told them I was here for my interview. They sent me into the Postmaster's office, and he informed me that they gave the job to someone else. Great, now I had to find a job.

I did a little construction, a little carpet cleaning, a few odd jobs and finally landed a position at a local paint store. I hated retail. I decided to use my GI bill and go back to college, hoping for a career in writing. I loved the writing part but didn't care for all the other classes I had to take. Finally, the Post Office sent me another letter for an interview. On December 7th, Pearl Harbor Day, 1972, I started my 32 year career as a city letter carrier. Shortly after that, using an $18,000 VA loan, Debbie and I bought our first home in Ft. Collins, a small but cozy house built, I think, in 1903.

I received a large and unexpected package from the Marine Corps. My uniforms I had stored in Okinawa finally caught up with me; too late for a "Junk on the bunk" and too moldy to save. I threw them away.

One day, in late June or early July, I was delivering a cul-de-sac on my route. It was a walking relay, and I was on the return leg back to my postal jeep when someone nearby set off a string of firecrackers. I hit the deck, and it took a few seconds before I realized that I was in no danger. Some of the mail had fallen out of my bag, and I hurriedly gathered it and hoped no one had seen my foolishness. I had

Epilogue

just delivered the next house when another string of firecrackers went off. I reacted as I had reacted before.

I stepped up my pace, and I made the P.O. proud and finished the relay almost at a run. While firecrackers continued to go off at intervals, I was able to limit my reactions to ducking. When I reached the jeep, I was sweating. I sat there for awhile until I got it together. That was always a problem around the 4th of July.

Debbie had one more "Dear John" to give me, and our divorce was final in March 1974.

I was totally distraught. I even went in to see the local Marine recruiter. I spent a lot of time visiting with him after work, and we became friends. I told him I was thinking about re-enlisting. He told me I was crazy. As a letter carrier, I made almost as much money as an officer did in the Corps.

I waited it out, and soon discovered that there are worse things than being alone. I was a single guy and had the "mall route," where a lot of pretty girls worked. I did my best to take advantage of my good fortune.

I decided to see if my hearing problem could be surgically corrected. I went to an audiologist, a pretty lady ear doctor. She put me in the testing booth. When I came out, she asked if I could hear her. I replied that I could. She said, in a voice a little louder than necessary,

"Scott, your hearing is really bad!"

I replied that I knew my hearing was bad. I just wanted to know if it could be fixed surgically. She said that it could not, but hearing aids would help.

I shook my head no.

She asked,

"Why not? Vanity?"

Nodding, I admitted, "I suppose."

She told me about a poster in the hearing center in Denver. It had a beautiful blond girl on it and asked, "How would you know if she said 'Yes?'"

I smiled and told her, "I just always assume they do."

With that, she told me to go away.

As painful as the day of my divorce was, April 30th, 1975, was far worse. I had the day off and sat alone in front of my TV, and watched the Marines evacuating the embassy in Saigon. I watched the images of Huey helicopters being pushed overboard off carrier decks. I saw the NVA tanks rolling down the streets of Saigon. I had been following the progress of the war in the last NVA offensive. Everyday, as the situation became worse, I expected that we would do something to insure that South Vietnam survived. I had ignored the writing on the wall, and not until that moment did I accept the fact that Nixon's "Peace with Honor" included sacrificing everything we had fought for. I heard the cries of 58,000 American dead scream, "Why?" I thought of the Korean platoon blown all to hell by the 500 pound booby trap. Through my closed eyes, I had a vision of

Epilogue

the first Viet Cong prisoner I saw executed. I was overcome with the suffering I had witnessed and not witnessed. Why indeed. I sat alone on my couch and cried like I had never cried before or since.

I felt duped. I was totally disgusted with the American people for their lack of support. I despised my government for committing so much to a bad cause. Before that day, I had always believed, "My Country, right or wrong." After that last day in April 1975, I trusted few people, and certainly not my government. I tended to hang out with veterans to seek a little understanding. I was always proud of my service with the Koreans and the Corps. "Ours is not to question why, ours is but to do or die!" Semper Fi!, OO RA!" We died by the thousands. But now, as we still try to tally the cost, we have the right to ask, "Why?"

I had kept in touch with my Anglico buddy, Joe Medina via telephone calls a couple of times a month. I was worried about Joe and how he was dealing with the "real world." As I was a single guy, I asked Joe and his wife to come out to Colorado and live with me. I wish they had. Shortly thereafter, I got a call from his wife. Joe was in jail on a murder charge. I briefly entertained the thought of trying to bust him out of jail, but quickly dismissed that as a stupid idea.

In 2010, I wrote a letter to Joe's parole board asking for leniency. I told them that service with the Koreans in Vietnam had exposed us to a lot of brutality. While I was able to cope, Joe was not. He was hoping to be released to a Veteran's program dealing with Post Traumatic Stress Disorder. I was sad to hear his parole had been denied. Joe was finally released in July of 2012, and we talk on the phone often. He has found God, and that will change everything.

It was shortly after I heard about Joe going to prison that I tried to write this story. I never got past the first chapter. I think that at that point in time, I was trying to forget. Now, 40 years later, I am trying to remember.

I have spent a large portion of my time since the war reading and studying war. With a few friends, we recreate battles in miniature. Not the Vietnam War, but we study in detail almost every other war the world has been in from the Napoleonic period through WWII. I think that understanding what others went through helps me to put my experience in perspective. I honor all soldiers throughout history. I scorn the leaders that put them in harms way for a bad cause. I want my country, and all countries for that matter, to pick their wars carefully; because, win or loose, the cost is horrific. And when we tally the dead, we must count all the dead, no distinction between friendly or enemy; they were all humans. They were all part of the cost of War. While killing another human being is sometimes justified, it should never be something to be proud of.

I enjoyed my job as a letter carrier. It was often a trying place, but with the aid of humor we dealt with it. I made many friends, both carriers and supervisors. But the USPS is not the USMC. Promotions were not based on merit as much as being a "yes man." There were only a few supervisors that would put themselves on the line for me like my Captain and First Sergeant did with the General. I do not blame the supervisors; it was just a bad system.

There were many times I felt totally lost, like a ship

Epilogue

without a rudder. And sometimes, my life showed it. I am sorry for anyone I hurt during those wandering times. For many years, the only thing I did right was to keep my job. A few good friends and a warm and supportive family helped me get through the rough spots. I am grateful that when I was not praying for myself, someone else was. I found my rudder when I married Jan. Shortly after that, I started praying again.

I am now retired. My pension is based on my thirty-two years with the Postal Service and the four years in the Marine Corps. I have heard complaints about being able to use those four years and the five points that were added to my clerk/carrier test. The same company that paid me to carry mail also paid me 22 cents an hour to get shot at and look for booby traps. Complain all you want. I still duck (more than everyone else I'm with) at a loud and unexpected noise, but I seldom hit the deck anymore. Because of my age it is harder to get back up. I have not had a bad dream about Vietnam for years. I have been married to my third wife, Jan, for twenty-five years. She convinced me to get hearing aids. I have three wonderful daughters and six awesome grandchildren that provide a lot of joy. I am a very solitaire person, and I thank my wife for her understanding, patience, love, support and, yes, even her guidance. She is my best bud.

After a particularly bad day in Vietnam, I remember telling Pete that if I made it home, I could be happy, even if I had to live in a sandbag bunker on my family's ranch. I still feel that way.

Vietnam and my life during those years are never far from my thoughts. It seems that the guy, Ron, in "Staging," who said to Johnny, "I don't think Leis is coming back," was partially right. Part of me didn't.

Epilogue

With Special Thanks

I would not have been able to write this book without the help of many people.

I wrote 83 letters home to my Sweet Ma and Dad during the 19 months I spent in Vietnam. Sweet Ma kept and protected them until just a few years ago. With the aid of those letters and photos, I was able to put all of those stories I can never forget into some kind of order.

Whenever I finished a chapter, I sent it via e-mail to my good friend, Jon Gilbert, whose opinion I greatly respect. He would return the chapter with suggestions and corrections, and always, and most importantly, encouragement and kind words. He gave me the most important thing I needed, encouragement.

Rex Molihan reminded me of the "stolen Air Force bunk beds." Joe Medina told me about the fate of the "Rocket LVT." Both Anglicomen contributed photos.

My wife, Jan, deserves the most thanks. She went through each chapter and approved the final draft. Often I would completely rewrite a chapter four or five times, yet she would reread and critique it each time. She accepted the fact that she would barely see me for days while I was working on this project. She has always stood by me, and I am forever grateful that she is my wife.

Scott Leis

Jan and Me in a recent photo.

There are people whose names I cannot remember. I remember the people, just not the names, and for that I apologize. It was an honor to serve with you all.

Semper Fi,

Scott Leis

www.ingramcontent.com/pod-product-compliance
Lightning Source LLC
Chambersburg PA
CBHW062152080426
42734CB00010B/1657